Relationship Impossible

By:

Stephanie Dolce

Introduction: Where we left off in Hello Love, Where's Cupid?

When I set out to write, "Hello Love, Where's Cupid," I had no idea that it would hit a lot of nerves with people, on both sides of the argument, in the matter of online dating. Not only did it hit a lot of nerves for those who "believe" in online dating, but I had many questions left to answer. Let's dive right in to what was discussed:

I talked about social media and relationships, when I mentioned the following:
"Here's the thing that most don't realize: In this age of social media, we get emotionally attached and connected to people we don't even know every day! The moment you start talking to someone every day, the moment you get their phone number, and the moment you talk about (and some promise) to meet -up, you are in a relationship with that person!
Some are friendships, yes, but I am talking about romantic relationships. So for those keeping the score at home, if what I described above sounds like you, congratulations, you are in an online relationship!"

Before social media came to be, our personal and professional relationships were separated by office walls. Now, through the use of social media, they aren't. I discussed how social media has effected our lives, for the good and for the bad. That then took us into the discussion on online dating and dating apps.

Misrepresenting yourself on a dating site or app is as easy as a click here and a click there.

See, when you meet someone either at a party or at a bar, you see the person for who the person is (look wise - no chance to use a fake picture) and for the most part, they aren't going to "make up a name" like they can and some do online. You can then actually get their name and do a background check on them yourself. With these dating sites, it's hard to know if they are being truthful as to who they really are. Another thing that you can decipher in person that you really cannot evaluate online is another person's sense of humor and connection. Reading a profile just isn't going to cut it. They can "say" they are the funniest thing around since Seinfeld, but saying it online and actually being funny in person are two different things. And some of the services the websites offer might backfire, causing users to overlook people they might be happy with while choosing people they really don't "match" up well with due to their answers and how they set up their profiles. At a party you may have two people to choose from, where as on the Internet dating sites, you have hundreds, thousands of different suitors to look over. I also broke the dating code, so to speak, by telling you how each site that "claimed" they had a scienific way of "matching" folks to the "correct" partner worked.

I then got into the conversation on what every site has failed to recognize is that there really is no way to successfully predict that a relationship will last, especially when the most crucial information is not collected:

A) Individual Characteristics of each partner which include personalities, attitudes and if each partner is relatively stable.
B) Quality of interactions – This can only be measured in person, not online. This includes how well the couple will communicate and also support each other.
C) Unforeseen Circumstances - This includes stress, financial problems, cultures, family issues, etc.

With this said, users beware that the only ultimate way to know if a relationship is going to last, is actual face-to-face interaction.
This then went into the stories about scams, lies, and the studies that show that online dating/ dating apps do not work the way they are intended to work, and I list those sites.

I also gave folks a little reminder, " Your future partner is not a link on a website, he or she is a human being."

Not only did I talk about the reasons why no one should be using these sites, I even gave you tips if you do want to try these sites. (What can I say, I care.)
I gave tips on how to win an ex back, even though I am totally against going back with an ex for this reason

alone: They are called an "ex" for a reason. Now, I am all for second chances, but you need to be extremely sure and confident that the relationship with your ex is worth it.

Also on the table of discussion, was if you are a guy who is looking for a relationship, I gave tips directly from the mouths of single women everywhere. I can tell you all that the first thing that bothers single women is the fact that men today have forgotten about chivalry.

Of course I had advice for women too when I said:
"I can't make people value me. All I can do is show them who I am, what I feel, and what I believe in. It's up to them to realize my worth. And what every woman needs to learn is the difference between what you're getting and what you deserve. Let the universe know this by the way you treat yourself."

My favorite chapter, and everyone's favorite chapter was 10 where I used some of my past relationships as lessons for what NOT to do. One of our best learning tools is looking back at our mistakes.
Each relationship has made me into who I am today. There is no way around that. I have not only grown as a person, but I have grown thicker skin, have taken more risks, and learned that life is short. Here are the lessons from that chapter that I wanted to pass along to all of you:

THE KEYS OF WHAT NOT TO DO:

a- Never judge anyone without getting to know them yourself.

b- Just because your boyfriend breaks up with you, doesn't mean that you need to date someone else right away to replace him. Learn to be alone and recover first, then date later.

c- You don't need to use your sexuality as a way to gain attention. Use it as a powerful tool to boost yourself confidence instead.

d- Never judge a book by its cover. Just because he looks like a Calvin Klein underwear model (and is one) does not mean that his personality is as "hot"

e-Don't give a guy that many chances. The truth is, if he wanted to be with you, he would be with you. Period.

f- If someone shows you their true colors, don't try and paint a different picture.

g- Finally, don't take a person you meet online at face value. It's easy for them to lie about who they are and if they are really using you in their little game. Google them. Find out if they are hiding anything. Always LISTEN to your instincts. When someone is using you, playing you, or things aren't adding up, your instincts will never lie to you.

To note the 2 relationships I briefly mentioned in the book: The 23 year old and the divorced dad who was in his 40s, those relationships went south.   The 23 year old was too scared to turn our relationship into something serious because he litterally was afraid of what his friends thought. Yes, guys are that immature and stupid. The 45ish divorced dad proved once and for all that NO ONE should get involved with a soon-to-be divorcee – RED FLAGS were everywhere and eventually were received, noted and dealt with in a timely manner.

Then we pivoted from that to of course talking about some serious topics in the dating world. When you hear the phrase, abusive relationship, usually domestic violence comes to mind, but emotional abuse is often minimized, yet it can leave deep and lasting scars. There are 3 different types of abuse that happen in relationships: 1) Domestic Violence 2) Rape and 3) Dating abuse.   These are topics that women try and aviod talking about becuase they are embarrassed to admit that they have been in an abusive relationship or they feel ashamed that they succumed to a man who triecked them into believing that he loved her by abusing her.

Abuse isn't always obvious.
Here are some red flags that everyone reading this should know and note:

- Call you names and put you down
- Call or text you throughout the day to check on you
- Keep you from friends or family
- Control your $

- Threaten to hurt you, himself/herself, your pet or loved one
- Hit, Kick, Push, Punch, Slap, Pinch, Choke or Bite you
- Destroy property or throw things
- Tell you who you can see or what job you can have
- Tell you how to dress
- Act overly jealous
- Withhold medication or health care
- Make you have sex or do sexual acts that you don't want to do
- Threaten to "out" you if you are gay or lesbian
- Constantly criticize
- Embarrass you
- Blame you for everything - including the abusive behavior

What usually happens after this happens the first time is that the victim makes statements like:

"My partner isn't violent all the time – they love me"
"Things will get better – they didn't mean it"
"Maybe it's *my* fault"
"I'm scared of what will happen if I leave them"

And the abuse continues.

Remember, most *relationships* start off with each person acting their best and seeing the other with rose-colored glasses. It never starts off on an abusive note.

There were many other topics we discussed in "Hello Love, Where's Cupid 2ⁿᵈ Ed" and the feedback from the book was tremedous. Which leads me to writing this follow up book, "Relatioship Impossible"

Here is a brief summary of the topics that will be discussed in the book- note that I am not mentioning EVERY topic.

A. How Covid 19 affected dating
B. How Dating apps and sites actually work
C. Social Media's Shallow Pitfalls
D. Athletes. Social Media, and Dating Apps
E. Myths: sexual myths, Out of My League Myths, etc.
F. The 7 Selfish Traits
G. How The Me Too Movement Changed Dating
H. The most dangerous / safe states for online dating

And much more.

Of course some of the topics that I have blogged about over the years, will be mentioned and some topics are those that trend on social media like the following:

Some guys have created this image of this "ideal" woman, so when regular women; regular, wonderful, real women fall short, they reject them. That way they never have to settle down and then everyone can still feel sorry about poor, lonely you.

I'm not saying that guys should just 'settle" but they aren't going to be happy if every time they discover a flaw in someone, they go to somebody else because every woman has her own flaws; no body is perfect. (And vice versa) Find that someone who makes you better, without trying to change who you are

Now before guys get their pants in a bunch, to be fair, I have seen guys do just this; they find a woman who is a down to Earth, "good woman" and then they find a flaw in her like, "Not pretty enough" or "too strong minded," so this way they avoid commitment because to them the "bad girls" are more attractive than the "good ones."

This is the reason that guys are hitting on girls on social media at a high rate and hooking up with girls left, center, and right on dating apps. They want the one and done relationships instead of the ones where they have to commit to one girl and "build a relatonship" with her. That takes time, energy, effort and work.

Men find bad sexy because the things they plan on doing to bad women are likewise "naughty." Bad is naughty and naughty is sexy. Good, on the other hand, sounds boring. Their definiton of sexy is misinterpreted. And then of course, these same guys think that "bad girls" are better in bed than "good girls" which has been proven to be a myth. The "bad girl" that men are so taken by at times isn't someone who is morally corrupt, but the challenge that a bad girl poses. One of the factors that makes a relationship with a bad girl fun yet short lived is the fact that most 'bad girls' ride big on the persona they create.

Take a close look on Instagram and you will get a sense of which girls have created a "fake persona," to gather attention, while the real, down to Earth girls show their true character online.

For a relationship to stay you need character. Personality is a superficial connect, whereas with character, you look for connection. So for a long term relationship, there has to be a shift from a superficial level to a deeper level – and that is why guys have to "test the road" with bad girls first before they settle down with a "good girl."

Then there is the saying, "Nice guys finish last."
The "nice" guy is the one who covers up his incompetence and lack of bravery by being patient and understanding. He's not really being nice: like every single male on the planet, he wants sex with you, but he takes backdoor and windows to enter your kingdom. There are also those guys that fall into this category: The too afraid to ask you out "nice guy" who will pass himself " just a friend" in hopes that you will one day see how great he is, therefore, being the one who asks him out. Then he romances the hell out out of you in hopes that he no longer will be in the "friend zone" but moved to the "boyfriend zone."

Of course the guy stuck in the friend zone will be thinking that the girl he has the hots for only wants to be with a, "bad boy." You know the type: The "bad boys" that some women are attracted to are usually nothing more than punks, thugs, and assholes who believe that society's rules do not apply to them. They are someone who does dangerously interesting stuff that differ from the so called *boring everyday of expected routine behavior* of other men.

If we say that "bad boys" are not outright criminals, but abusive, arrogant, manipulative men. Well, such men don't usually show this side of their personality to a woman they want to attract. They are predators, their purpose is to attract potential "prey", not to scare it off. Abusers and manipulators don't appear as such until the "prey" has fallen into the trap. So, we cannot say that women are attracted to the abusers or manipulators as such. Women are attracted to the personality they want to show. The issue is actually that abusers and manipulators find it easier to appear confident and comfortable in their skin. On one hand, because they can play any role they want and usually have a lot of practice doing it. On the other hand, because they really don't care about other people, they don't really care if they succeed with one particular woman or not. They just move to the next target.

The majority of women are not attracted to "bad boys" because they are "bad", but because it is easier for such men to make initial contact and take it from there. "Bad boy" romances, being more forbidden/against norm/full of regret stories/full of drama/etc, are simply better topics for gossip than a nice, normal, quiet, healthy romance- think about all the movies, TV shows, and books you have read and tell me which types people prefer. Of course, when you turn on Hallmark Channel, the girl always gets the boy she wants and the bad boy turns good at the end, which in reality is usually never the case.

Good girls, bad boys, nice guys, to bad girls, there is always going to be sterotypes of how people behave when it comes to sex, romance and relationships. What it should always come down to is finding the right partner. One of the ways to do that is to find someone you can talk to. Being able to talk with your partner about important topics is probably worth more than physical beauty, money or power. You might disagree at times, but by being able to be open and honest with each other, leads you to fulfill what you want out of the relationship. When you make each other feel loved and emotionally fulfilled, the rest starts to fall into place.

But let me warn you on this note, being alone and being lonely are not the same thing. And nothing is as unhealthy and dispiriting as being in a bad relationship.

This is another reason why dating apps are not good for mental health as well as your physical health. First and foremost, A group of psychologists in the Netherlands have discovered that we have a tendency to gradually close ourselves off when dating online. In other words, the more dating profiles people see, the more likely they are to reject them. The study shows that the endless stream of options can increase feelings of dissatisfaction and pessimism about finding a partner, which in turn leads to rejecting potential mates. Thanks to Dating Apps there are more possibilities to meet new partners than ever before, yet at the same time there have never been more people single in western society. This could be simply because the study found that both men and women tend to focus on the picture more than any other part of the online dating profile, but women view each profile for a longer amount of time than men do. Women spend an average of 84 seconds on each profile while the men spent an average 54 seconds on each profile.

The male participants made more snap judgments based on a photo, while the female participants displayed a more methodical approach to online dating. But sadly other studies have shown that depression symptoms and social anxiety are associated with greater use of mobile dating applications among women. If men are judging the women on these apps by appearance, and some women are not "appearing" attractive, then they are not getting too many "swipes." This is due to the fact that socially anxious people tend to avoid asking others out on dates, fearing that they will be rejected or be negatively evaluated.

Stuck at home, due to the pandemic, dating has become an endless scroll, sifting through hundreds of pictures and profiles. Not only does this lead to more depression and anxiety, it leads to massive social problems across the board when it comes to dating apps. For starters, dating experiences can differ widely based on a person's gender identity and sexual orientation. A single man may say his biggest worry about online dating is meeting a catfisher, while a single woman may say her biggest worry is being sexually assaulted or harassed.

The free-for-all atmosphere can be particularly overwhelming to the average single woman because, taken as a whole, straight men tend to be more proactive about liking and messaging women on dating sites and apps. If you are not into sports, in particular, baseball, then you missed the story about Jared Porter and how he harassed a female reporter through texting and texted her lewd photos of his junk. This is another problem that women face on a daily basis as they put themselves out there on dating apps as well as social media.

There was a study done recently that found 80 percent of the men and almost 50 percent of the women reported receiving a "dick pic." 90 percent had received one without asking for it. "This includes 90.7% of women — 90.7% of heterosexual, 91.3% of lesbian, and 90.8% of bisexual women — and 87.1% of men — 88.1% of gay men and 82.1% of bisexual men. heterosexual men primarily send unsolicited images of their genitals to women in the hopes of receiving either similar images or sexual interactions in return. But the new findings suggest that such images rarely provoke the intended response. Women of all sexual identities reported predominantly negative reactions. The researchers found that 50% of women who received unsolicited genital images reported feeling "grossed out" and 46% felt "disrespected." There's a lot of work that needs to be done in the communication world, and one of them is the fact that men think this behavior is still acceptable in 2021, when women clearly are trying to tell men to stop behaving in this fashion. When will they finally listen?

While now it might be hard to imagine a world without this virtual matchmaking, in reality these apps are still fresh, which means that studies into the impact they've had on our mental health and the studies that have been done over the last five or so years are starting to show that these dating apps don't bode well for mental well being. Research by psychologist Barry Schwartz in his book, "Paradox of Choice,"has shown that even though we like having more options when making a decision, we are less satisfied with our choice the more options we have. (which was written in my first book FYI) For users confronted by this seemingly overwhelming array of options you can understand why a reluctance to settle may develop, especially when a new round of matches are only a swipe away- which is the reason for people staying single longer and not getting into a commuted relationship. What dating apps do to singles is that . instead of allowing a connection to happen organically they worry about making a mistake or missing out on the one when the one could be right in front of them. In other terms, singles are looking for perfection which does not exist.

(Note: There is some foul language in this book)

Chapter Index

Chapter 1: Covid 19, Dating and Sexual Assault

The pandemic literally has had people thinking about life and death on a regular basis for the past year. This causes people to reflect on what gives their life meaning – relfection that could make people prioritize the search for a serious relationship. Finding love can be challenging all in it's own right, now try to do it in a pandemic.

Being forced to stay at home and working remotely has made some singles more determined than ever to find the love of their life. It has taken Zoom meetings and Facetime to an entirely new level. IT also though has not shyed some folks away from actually hooking up either. People were meeting up, cuddling, making out and having sex with new partners, often weighing their emotional and physical needs against safety concerns of Covid-19 thanks to dating apps and social media but on the whole, did Covid 19 really change dating as we have known it?

During this time, there have been numerous polls done on dating during this Covid-19. Here is a sample of some of those polls:

45% said that they now think physical attraction is less important because of Covid.
 I find this one hard to believe since we know that phyiscal chemistry is important and physical attraction is

onle one piece of the puzzle. A piece that is often overemphasized in online dating and social media.
(Note: It's relatively of lesser importance of long term relationship satifisfaction)

59% are now open to a wider ranger of potential partners due to Covid-19.

And that's not all. 43% said that because of Covid-19 they feel less connected to their matches knowing that in person meetings were more limited.

The pandemic, at least by some metrics, has been great for business. Dating.com reported that global online dating was up 82% during early March. As states across the country began rolling out stay-at-home orders in March 2020, Bumble saw a 26% increase in the number of messages sent on its platform, Tinder saw the length of "conversations " rise by 10-30% and elite dating app Inner Circle saw messages rise 116% over that same time period. So the dauntinig question is simply, why? Why were people who were giving up on dating apps and online dating, all of a sudden running to it in high numbers when the quarantines started?

The answer can be as simple as seeing dating apss were a way to solve the problem of loneliness that happened to be compounded because of Covid-19.
Studies have shown that when daters gp through large numbers of profiles, they pay less attention to each individual potential match, resulting in poor choices.

Viewing large number of matches at once also causes daters to enter a rejection mindet in which they become choosier as they go photo to photo- focusing on looks not how each match could be or couldn't be a potential parnter.

Slowing down the courtship process could mitigate some of the problems with online dating. Relationships off line develop slowly from friendship as online relationships have little or no time at all to develop at a slow pace because there's pressure to turn it into a romantic relationship immediately. Which is also why this next poll isn't surprising. 25% of singles reconnected with an ex-partner during the lockdown and 10% of those people actually did the "no-no" and rekindled the relationship.

After talking to several dating app users, I have little doubt dating apps feel different in the age of social distancing. In-person dates have been replaced with in-app video chats and FaceTime calls. Chatting with others for entertainment or companionship, not the desire for long-term commitment has become much more common.

Stuck at home, due to the pandemic, dating has become an endless scroll, sifting through hundreds of pictures and profiles. Not only does this lead to more depression and anxiety, it leads to massive social problems across the board when it comes to dating apps. For starters, dating experiences can differ widely based on a person's gender identity and sexual orientation. A single man may say his biggest worry about online dating is meeting a catfisher, while a single woman may say her biggest worry is being sexually assaulted or harassed.

The free-for-all atmosphere can be particularly overwhelming to the average single woman because, taken as a whole, straight men tend to be more proactive about liking and messaging women on dating sites and apps. If you are not into sports, in particular, baseball, then you missed the story about Jared Porter and how he harassed a female reporter through texting and texted her lewd photos of his junk. This is another problem that women face on a daily basis as they put themselves out there on dating apps as well as social media.

There was a study done recently that found 80 percent of the men and almost 50 percent of the women reported receiving a "dick pic." 90 percent had received one without asking for it. "This includes 90.7% of women — 90.7% of heterosexual, 91.3% of lesbian, and 90.8% of bisexual women — and 87.1% of men — 88.1% of gay men and 82.1% of bisexual men. heterosexual men primarily send unsolicited images of their genitals to women in the hopes of receiving either similar images or sexual interactions in return. But the new findings suggest that such images rarely provoke the intended response. Women of all sexual identities reported predominantly negative reactions. The researchers found that 50% of women who received unsolicited genital images reported feeling "grossed out" and 46% felt "disrespected." There's a lot of work that needs to be done in the communication world, and one of them is the fact that men think this behavior is still acceptable in 2021, when women clearly are trying to tell men to stop behaving in this fashion. When will they finally listen?

Obviously not soon enough. Again, three in four women say they've been sent pictures of men's genitalia without their consent; in social media chats, for example, while online-dating, or even in public, through sharing functions like Apple's Air Drop. Results also showed that men who admitted they had sent a picture without being asked showed a greater degree of narcissism and sexism. On Reddit, there was a questions posed by this women where she asked men directly if and why they had ever sent a dick pic. The men were allowed to answer anonymously. The thread exploded and different motives were given. These ranged from a desire for validation and a confidence boost due to low self esteem, to the goal of arousal, to some kind of probability calculation. They hoped, at some point, a woman would engage with them.

This behavior is often based on men's misinterpretation of women's sexual interest. For some, the thought of sexual rejection is the main source of excitement, for others, it's exactly what they fear. The study suggests that men with a heightened fear of rejection use dick pics to gauge whether their naked bodies are considered attractive, figuring an online interaction might be less painful than in real life.

Now let's look at this from a woman's point of view. When matches become potential perpetrators rather than would-be suitors. I get tons of messages from guys that want to chat. Usually my go-to excuse not to chat to I tell him I am busy, which really isn't a lie. This one particular guy one day then asked me if he could send me something. Instantly an image came through of his penis. Then he asked how he could video himself masturbating. I instantly reported him first, and then block him. Any time a guy asks, "Want to chat?" My instant reaction is NO. They are not looking to "chat" they are looking for some sort of sexual affirmation which is deeply disturbing.

Online abuse is NOT okay. It NEVER has been and it NEVER will be okay. The other problem with social media and dating apps is the fact that when a woman kindly asks a guy NOT to send those pictures ever again, men become even more abusive and defensive. Men will call the woman a prude, a bitch, even a hoe based on whatever outfit she has posed in her selfie, and accuse her of not knowing what a real dick looks like. They tell her that she needs to see a good one so she will appreciate what a "real man" is.
If you stopped me in the street and whipped out your penis, I could report you and have you arrested for indecent assault. Why would it be OK for you to do it online?

I work online to inspire and empower other girls and women to be their own boss, to start their own empires, mind you. I am a busy gal who dedicates time to helping others, engaging in actual conversations, and to creating my legacy that I wish to leave behind. I am not online to receive pictures of your penis.

Dating apps are no different than social media apps these days either. Guys pull the same shit on both of them. With the pandemic, there's another layer of expectations and judgment.

In one corner you had some folks who were proponents of staying inside and minimizing contact with other people while in the other corner you had people who were traveling everywhere like there's nothing going on. Since folks were missing many of our everyday interactions, like socializing at the office or going out with friends, people turned to dating apps to wipe away the feelings of isolation and loneliness.

But Covid was no excuse for men to behave like pigs on social media and on dating apps. Most took advantage of this situation and more and more women were being violated online then ever before!

With everyone now working from home, the toxic workplace environment moved online. This generally refers to when a person with some form of power, such as a manager, uses it to target another individual and cause mental harm. Working from home has blurred the line between professional and personal behavior. Thanks to all the technology today, there are many online tools that are used to harass women.

Online sexual harassment falls in two categories:
Under the first category, the victim receives emails, texts or instant messages that contain sexually explicit words or photos from their harasser. The harasser may proposition the victim or send inappropriate images or videos of themselves or others.

The second category of online sexual harassment includes behaviors such as:

- Comments or rumors about the victim's sexuality
- Comments or rumors about the victim's sexual activities
- Sharing sexually explicit photos without consent
- Using sexual or gender-based derogatory terms to describe the victim

People may post this content on their social media pages or online forums or send it to others via email, text message or other digital application. While "traditional" sexual harassment usually involved one perpetrator and one or more victims, online sexual harassment may include numerous folks ganging up on one victim. Here's where it gets tricky.

37% of online dating users say someone on a dating site or app continued to contact them even after he or she said they weren't interested in communicating. Question though, was did those 37% TELL them to scat? Communication lacks on dating apps and social media. So many folks are afraid to tell a person to go away so they just ignore the messages. And whether or not you knew the person, but especially if you worked together, this makes working whether in person or online even more uncomfortable then ever before.

With 1 in 5 people meeting their partner at work, the public opinion on dating coworkers has shifted dramatically in the past few years. A 2015 survey found that just 5 percent of respondents believe office romances are never appropriate, down from 9 percent in 2011. And more respondents than ever (29%) said all romantic connections in the workplace are appropriate— including those between managers and their direct reports. Another survey in 2018 found that office romances are at a 10-year low, with 36 percent of workers reporting dating a coworker, down from 41 percent a year earlier.

The most common way for office romances to begin is working in the same department (36 percent) or in nearby offices or cubicles (28 percent). To follow are happy hours and office parties (26 percent) and working on the same project (21 percent). 34 percent of business professionals believe that social media platforms and productivity tools have made it easier for colleagues to pursue romantic interests in one another. It also has made it easier to sexually harass others too.

Then came the #MeToo movement which has rightly brought sexual harassment to the forefront of the American conversation. But it's also had a major effect on public opinion about workplace dating overall. The rise of online dating, #MeToo and COVID-19 have all contributed to a decline in office romance.

While the COVID-19 has certainly played a role in the office romance decline, the workforce had already kissed workplace flirtations goodbye well before coronavirus lock downs. Most companies don't ban infra-office romances, but some have certainly considered taking that approach. Yet, such measures can wind up backfiring by creating a culture of secrecy. Yet, failed workplace relationships can present a minefield of human resource problems that, if not handled properly, can really made folks today think twice about having any romance with a co-worker. 'Love Contracts' or 'Consensual Relationship Agreements' are more commonly used by employers to get employees to confirm that the relationship in question is consensual and provide a level of protection against future claims relating to sexual harassment and discrimination are actually common today.

A recent survey taken before the #Metoo movement found that 33 percent of unsuccessful workplace dating relationships resulted in at least one person being terminated. An additional 17 percent resulted in departmental transfers, and 5 percent led to litigation. No matter how you cut it, dating someone at work can be career ending. Some folks are willing to take that risks while others turned to dating apps instead. This is why all the major digital platforms have their work cut out to address the online harassment of women that has now become commonplace.

Whether women are sexually harassment and assaulted online or in person, If women want to end the culture of sexual violence, we have to hold ourselves to the same standard of behavior we want men to abide by.

There can't be "rules" for men to follow and a whole different set of "rules" for women. When women are being raped and assaulted, government, police and public figures say 'women, need to change their behaviors and to do something different'.

Why are women supposed to change their lives and their behaviors for sex offenders?

As discussed in, "Hello Love, Where's Cupid 2nd Ed," We live in a society that teaches women not to get raped, instead of teaching men, do not rape."

And as a woman I can tell you all the advice I have been given over the years to "protect myself." Always stick to well-lit streets. If possible, let someone know when you are coming home and the route you are taking and always be alert in your surroundings, so don't use earphones or handheld devices, etc. While I'm sure the advice is well intended, it's very problematic. This narrative puts the victim at fault, rather than the criminal. What if we could stop sexual violence before it happens? We have to start teaching men to respect a woman's right to say no to sexual activity.

No mean No. It doesn't mean maybe or try asking me again later. NO means NO.

{ Sources: CBS and NBC news /Forbes and NPR}

Chapter 2: How Dating Apps and Sites Actually Work

Now that most of the lockdown rules have been lifted, online dating / dating apps are returning to it's regular scheduled programming, with singles and married folks looking for that one night hook up. But what makes people first, go on a app, and then swipe? Do the apps work against you or for you?

The first location-based apps changed that. Grindr was launched in 2009, and it helped single, often anonymous gay men link up by searching for other active users within a specific geographic radius. Then, with the launch of Tinder in 2012, smartphone-owning people of all sexualities could start looking for love, or sex, or casual dating in their area, and it quickly became the most popular platform on the market.

Today, there is no shortage of dating apps available. The most notorious hookup app, especially among the younger folks, remains Tinder, with its popular "swiping" feature: online daters use right or left swipes to "like" or "dislike" photos of other users (if each of you swipes right on the other person — it's a match). Tinder now reports 1.6 billion swipes and 26 million matches a day.

Bumble is America's second favorite app, and its swiping feature comes with a catch: Anytime there's a match, only users who identify as women can text first. Some apps like Hinge removed the swiping feature entirely, and instead, users spark a conversation with a person of interest by liking their photo or commenting on a prompt in their profile, such as "a life goal of mine" or "the most spontaneous thing I've ever done."

Kelly, 27, has been using Hinge and Bumble for three years, and says that for her, getting matches is easy. The hard part? "The annoying small talk." She goes on to say, "Don't ask me what my favorite color is because I'm going to ghost you."

And ghosting is made easier with a seemingly bottomless list of potential matches on the apps that can make it seem as if there is always someone better than the current date. If you detect a flaw (no matter how minor) that makes you suddenly lose interest, there are still plenty of suitors awaiting in your phone.
The more options you have the more superficial your criteria will be.

So, how do these dating apps really work?

Since users don't know which swipe will bring the reward of a match, apps like Tinder use a variable ratio reward schedule, which means that your matches will be randomly dispersed. It's the same reward system used in slot machines in Las Vegas. Dating sites are in the business of keeping users swiping, looking at their advertisements (on Tinder, you might accidentally swipe right on an ad), and paying monthly fees for extra features that should supposedly make finding matches easier, such as Bumble Boost (which costs up to $25 a month and adds 24 hours to the time users have to break the ice with their match).

In the midst of the swiping fever in 2015, Tinder began to limit the amount of daily right swipes to 100 for users who don't buy into their premium service, Tinder Plus (up to $30 a month).

Even though Tinder, OkCupid, eHarmony have managed to keep the secret behind their matchmaking process a secret, researchers at Cornell University have cracked that can wide open.

These days most online dating apps use their AI algorithm to match new users on the following factors initially –

1. The agreeableness level
2. Closeness preference
3. Romantic passion range
4. Extroversion or Introversion level
5. Importance of spirituality
6. The level of optimism or happiness

In addition to these criteria, the algorithm then adds on the new user's location, height, religion information to draw matches for users.

So, you can see that the algorithm polls in all this information and draws in matches that are closest to the new user's preference. Hence, you can thank math for that lovely date you had last Saturday.

So, technically, yes, there are ways to play with the algorithm but, it is never advised to do so. Because, even if it is preferential dating math, being yourself online is the best way to be. Algorithms of dating apps expect their users to use their applications genuinely. Don't try shortcuts.

One of the things that all these sites have in common is this: They insert fear that unless you are on their dating site you will NEVER find your "soul-mate." They tug at your heartstrings to make you believe that you mate is on the other side of your computer screen.

Research done by Villanova University, Northwestern University and Psychological Science in the Public Interest (PSPI), back this up.

Here is a fact: Romantic relationships can begin any time and any where. You can be at school, church, a coffee shop, playing a sport, or be at a friend's party. Sometimes though people go through stretches where they hit a rut in the romance department and freak out. Most likely when you hit a certain age you freak out more than "usual" because you have relatives, friends and even strangers giving you the sad, pathetic look because you are "single" and that automatically makes you "unhappy" or "lonely."

Lets be honest here, just because you are single doesn't mean that qualifies you as a lonely, unhappy person, where you are going to now be the next owner of seventy-two cats to compensate for your single-hood.

eHarmony and Match.com claim that their mathematical formula really identify pairs of singles who are especially likely to have a successful romantic relationship. With that said, how do they know how two people will interact once they have been matched? Do they check marital stability and marital satisfaction, not only marriage itself after two people from their sites get hitched? What are divorce rates for sites Match and eHarmony? Do their claims that "1 in 5 relationships start online," and "We've conducted years of extensive research and know what makes relationships last," true or are these dating sites all part of an elaborate hoax pulling at a person's heartstrings?

According to Pew Research Center, larger shares of Americans who are currently using dating sites or apps or who have done so in the past year say the experience left them feeling more frustrated (45 percent) than hopeful (28 percent), citing among other things lack of personal and emotional connections, safety concerns, focus on hookups and "too many options."

As an example, the 10 million active daily users of the popular online dating application Tinder are on average presented with 140 partner options a day. While one may expect this drastic increase in mating opportunities to result in an increasing number of romantic relationships, the opposite has occurred.

Online daters indeed became less satisfied with the search proves as the number of profiles they look at get into the hundreds or even thousands.

34

This is called, choice overload where people undermine their ability to make a good, well thought out decision due to having way too many options available to them. This has been proven that when looking through thousands of dating profiles becomes painful, this starts to decrease their level of interest and it might also undermine making a relationship work once offline.

Having extensive choice can have various adverse effects, such as paralysis (i.e., not making any decision at all) and decreased satisfaction . In fact, it seems that people generally experience *less* benefits when they have more choice. This observation is reminiscent of the basic economic principle of *diminishing returns* in which each unit that is sequentially added to the production process results in less profits.

There is some evidence that having more choice in the domain of dating also has negative consequences. For example, when asked to pick the best partner, access to more partner profiles resulted in more searching, more time spent on evaluating bad choice options, and a lower likelihood of selecting the option with the best personal fit. Likewise, when a choice set increases, people end up being less satisfied with their ultimate partner choice and more prone to reverse their decision. The adverse effects of choice overload are also mentioned in articles in popular media mentioning phenomena such as "Tinder fatigue" or "dating burnout"

Study after study found that online dating will set off a *rejection mind-set*, leading people to become increasingly likely to reject partners to the extent that they have been presented with more options.

Every dating site has an algorithm that they use in matching people together. It is not "fate" that helps you meet the person, it is artificial intelligence.
Do scientific algorithms — including those used by sites like eHarmony, PerfectMatch and Chemistry
to match people according to similarities — can really lead to better and more lasting relationships?
The answer is no. There are certain properties of online datieHarmony's system is flawed because it relies on conclusions from married couples and a fundamental premise that similar people will be happy together in the long-term. But married couples often project similarities onto one another and adopt similar interests over time, ng that actually work against love-seekers, the researchers found, making it no more effective than traditional dating for finding a happy relationship.
so those are the results of a relationship rather than what inspires them in the first place. Match and the other apps use the same type of recommendation system used by Netflix or Facebook, taking your past behaviors (and the behavior of others) into account to predict what you'll like next. To understand how many dating app algorithms work, it's useful to compare them to Netflix. The streaming service's "trending now" category surfaces content other people enjoy. Many dating app algorithms work similarly, surfacing profiles popular with other

users. The problem is a popular profile isn't the same thing as a good individual match.

Netflix also relies on users with similar viewing histories to generate content suggestions. Dating apps do the same thing, surfacing profiles based on other people's swipe habits. If you swiped right on Harry and Sally swiped right on Harry, you might like someone else Sally swiped right on. Once again, the algorithms aren't tailored to individual users, but lumping people together in a fairly superficial manner. Algorithms can take into account how frequently you log on, how often you swipe right, how you strike up a conversation, and even how often you exchange numbers. Users often self-sabotage without even realizing it. On Bumble, if you simply say 'Hi,' Bumble learns that you're not making an effort, so it sets you back a notch. Before you know it, the algorithm makes a ton of bad assumptions based on your behavior and you're stuck in a never-ending cycle of undesirable matches.

Despite longer questionnaires and bios, matchmaking sites like OkCupid aren't any better. The truth is none of these sites *really* has any idea what they're doing— otherwise they'd have a monopoly on the market.

{ Source: Wired / BBC / Vox}

And it gets worse from here:

One study published in Science Advances found that among men who use dating apps, when deciding on what kind of woman they want to date many will choose a woman younger than them rather than a peer their own age. The study found that a when it came to age women typically found men up to the age of 50 very desirable. On the other hand most men only found women desirable up to the age of.... 18. (Yikes!)

Considering that women who are 18 are just one year up from being a teenager it's a little bit concerning and creepy.

Not only are the findings of the research disheartening for women genuinely trying to date through these apps but it is also majorly concerning that so many men across different apps and sites are messaging teenagers. { Source: Discover / Her / }

New research from William Chopik, an associate professor in the Michigan State University Department of Psychology, and Dr. David Johnson from the University of Maryland, finds that people's reason for swiping right is based primarily on attractiveness and the race of a potential partner, and that decisions are often made in less than a second. While attractiveness played a major role in participants' decisions to swipe left or right, race was another leading factor. Users were significantly more likely to swipe on users within their same race.

A growing body of research suggests that readers of your profile assess your attentiveness and intelligence based on grammar, spelling, and typos. Two recent studies analyzed the roles played by writing in online profiles. While this plays a small factor, a lot of people try to claim that if you post good pictures, have a good headline, have a well written profile and write a lot of people you'll do well. Yes, good pictures help, but you have to have a certain level of appealing looks for those pictures to work. Here's the reason why pictures are 99.99% the reason people swipe right or left.

First: On (most definitely all) dating websites and dating apps the first thing that a prospective partner has the chance to see about you is your face. Your profile picture to be more accurate. Not your interests, not the schools you went to, not the travels you made. It will be your photo.

Second: **NO ONE**, in the history of online dating as ever said "I don't find him (or her) particularly attractive, but I will check the rest of his profile to see if I feel a connection with him through his interests, life philosophy, past experiences, etc."

Third: If they like your profile picture enough they will check the rest of your profile as well BUT they will start with the other pictures. And only after checking all of them and deciding that you are attractive enough, will they check the rest of your profile.

HighSpeedInternet.com recently published a list revealing the online dating safety statistics for each state. The statistics are compiled using factors like violent crime rates, STD rates from the Centers for Disease Control and Prevention, sex education data and more.

At the top of the list of the most dangerous states for online dating are Alaska at number one, Nevada at number two and California at number three and North Carolina at number four.

So, how did New York measure up?

Not so well. The Empire State took the ninth spot on the list, putting it in the top 20th percentile of the nation's most dangerous states for online dating. The study states that the safest states for online dating are Maine, West Virginia, and Vermont.

STD rates have spiked nationwide over the past five years, and many experts blame online-dating apps for enabling easy hookups that spread infections faster.

Though Maine takes the lead in safety overall, West Virginia—ranked the second-safest state for online dating —is the least likely state for residents to get STDs, according to the Centers for Disease Control and Prevention.

We will continue our talk about ST D's later on.

Recently, I asked about 500 guys " What are your biggest frustrations with online/dating apps? Here, in a nutshell is how most men feel about online-dating:

- **Double standard with starting a conversation**

There's an expectation that as a dude, you need to start off a conversation with a new match in some great way. Whether it's using funny pick up lines, a thoughtful question based on their profile, or something else interesting, you *need* to do it or risk **never** getting a response. On the flip side, most women that ever reach out to me start off the conversation with "Hi", "Heyy", "hello", or some boring variant like that. *What the fuck is that?* So lame!

- **Randomly stops responding**

This is an annoying thing about online dating. You can be trying to get to know someone and have a decent conversation but then they just randomly stop responding. I even have women reach out and say "Hi" and I respond with hello and some question based on their profile and.. they never respond! That shit is stupid. Why reach out in the first place?!

- **All profile pics are group photos**

This gets annoying because it is nice to know how the person actually looks. Sometimes, like on Tinder, it's easy to choose to match them because everyone in a pic seems attractive, but often that's not the case and so you need to call in Scooby Doo and the gang to help sort out the mystery.

- **All profile pics use some Snapchat filter**

This is also annoying because of the false advertising it results in. I have gone out with women who look decent thanks to the filters but in person were quite different. Looks aren't everything, but if you cannot be honest with something like your appearance, what else will you be dishonest about?

- **People that use old photos that look way different than they currently do**

I've been burned by this quite a few times and I'm sure many can relate to this. It is also pretty self explanatory why this gets annoying.

- **Online dating is shallow as fuck**

For the most part, many online dating apps have got a swipe and match approach based on brief profiles with photos, though some allow for more detailed profiles (like OkCupid). This approach allows for minimal information about yourself which is shallow on its own. Add to that the fact that most success tends to come from witty, humorous, high level conversation instead of really getting to know someone on the app. This makes you end up going on dates with people who honestly you could have weeded out easily by asking a few questions about them on the app.. if only you had the chance!

- **Fake Profiles**

While many of these profiles are pretty easy to spot, since they tend to use model looking photos, it is still such an annoyance to have to put up with this shit.

- **Everyone is a traveler**

Look, I know many people on online dating apps/sites are part of the people who tend to inflate their life a bit, but damn this gets annoying. I swear, most women I see have photos of them from traveling all over and they talk about how they need someone who will travel and all that shit. I'm just like, there's no fucking way you all have money and free time lying around to travel so frequently. I smell a lot of parents' money and either you are unemployed or inflating how much you actually travel with old photos.

- **Rejection factory**

There is a major Catch-22 to online dating from a male perspective. In order to receive a response, you must A) flood the platform with a huge number of messages B) Write messages of sufficient quality to attract a profile view.

The result is a system where you are obligated to invest huge amounts of time with a resulting pay-off of overwhelming, crushing rejection.

When I started, I would send out 20–25 small paragraph long, unique messages per night. Of those, I'd probably receive one response every four to five days.

That is a base response rate of around 1 in 100. That's not dates. That's just replies.

I don't blame women. They are often flooded with messages to the point that it is impossible to respond to all of them.

Still, that is a lot of rejection. If you kept that up for a month, that would average about 396 rejections. Systematized and laid out in neat spread sheet form on the sent messages panel.

Now, it was the ladies turn. I asked 500 ladies this question: IN online-dating/ dating apps, what are the small, subtle clues that will make you reject a guy instantly? Here are those answers:

- Starting a conversation by demanding that I post more pictures. That's a *hard* pass. I don't even know this person and they're already demanding pictures.
- Starting a conversation with complaints about women. Nope.
- Aesthetic requirements on the profile (eg: no fat chicks, no tall chicks, etc.) Even when I fit the requirements, that's a hard pass. My brains are more important than what I look like, and that needs to be what someone is willing to engage, or I'm really not interested.
- Any "for a girl" statements. (eg: You're smart for a girl. You're nerdy for a girl. You're aggressive for a girl, etc.) That tells me way, way too much about the person I'm talking to, and none of it is good.

- Any "crazy bitch" comments on the profile or in conversation. (eg: Commentary about your crazy ex, or jokes about how crazy women are, or bragging about how you just manage to attract the crazy ones.)
- Bragging about yourself. I don't care how many toys you have. I don't care how much you earn at work. I don't care what names you can drop, and if you're desperate to tell everyone about it, I know we aren't going to get along, because it matters to you and it turns me off.
- Starting a conversation with how much you need to get laid, or how lonely you are.
- Demanding details outside my profile within the first few conversations.
- Demanding trust before earning it.
- Starting a conversation with sexting and dick pics. Seriously, does that *ever* work?
- Nothing on the profile that indicates the willingness to read or things on the profile that make it clear the person hates reading. Oddly, this requirement gets me the most shit from people, despite the fact that it's the equivalent of wanting a partner that has a hobby you share.
- Political conspiracy theories on the profile or in conversation. Nope.
- Literary references on profile that are shallow or terribly written political propaganda.
- Rudeness. If I can manage to be polite in messages, so can you.

- Religiosity. If you are religious, keep it to yourself. Don't open contact between the two of us with your religion, and don't talk my ear off about it. It's your religion, not mine, and I don't want to be converted, so seriously: keep it to yourself.
- Copious misspellings and bad grammar. Everyone messes up from time to time, but people who appear to completely disdain the built-in spell check and basic grammar rules are a pass for me. It would drive me crazy (yes, yes, women are petty.)

After reading the answers it is true, dating profiles present us with only fairly superficial information about our potential matches, which means that we are not seeing or being presented with the person as a whole. Consequently, the information which we glean from an online profile gives us very little to go on in determining how someone may actually behave in real life. It may be argued that online dating companies really don't want us to meet our soulmates; they would rather us keep coming back again and again to use their sites and this way they make more money.

The choice is yours, but just note that online dating is not the universal remedy.

Chapter 3: Social Media's Shallow Pitfalls

Social media can be great for relationships, as it keeps us connected, but it also does many other things that can tear us apart. First and foremost, there's a fine line between what's appropriate to post for a relationsip (especially when it's new) and what's not. As I wrote in, "Hello Love, Where's Cupid, the 2nd Ed," Thanks to social media, today's generation and those who have been accustomed to it, never really

break up with anyone anymore. The word, "boyfriend" to a girl/woman today, has many different

meanings- or if you ever have watched the "Big Bang Theory," as *Sheldon Cooper* described Amy;

"She's a girl and she's my friend, but she's not my girlfriend," is the way some people see friends of the opposite sex.

Ex's of all kinds today can be ANYWHERE online and seeing one pop up on your time-line on Facebook, Instagram or Twitter, can be just as heart-wrenching as bumping into them at the grocery store or on the street. It is because of this that I now use the term "ex-commodity." Cutting ties is no longer easy and for some they don't want it to be, so hence, they now have become a "commodity" that we "may" get to use or have back in our lives at one point again. We hang on to our "ex-commodity" like the way little kids hold on to a lollipop tightly!

People follow their "ex-commodity" on social media for many reasons;

– The ex you follow so you can spy on their new girlfriend
– the ex you follow so you know how to win him back
– the ex you follow so you can make sure he is not bad-mouthing you
– the ex you follow so you can watch his life deteriorate because he broke up with you

And if you think that there are no people who actually "block" their ex's but use their friends accounts to spy on their ex's page, then I have a bridge to sell you! (It's too bad we can find a way to permanently block some of those ex-commodities from our minds, hearts and really our lives.)

At face value, social media may seem like merely another tool to get to know a person. In reality, Facebook and Instagram portray a distorted, disjointed, and altogether imaginary version of ourselves. (It's the fake person, the fake stories, and the fake lives that post merely because we want to look perfect in the eyes of the public.)

The problem with falling in love with someone's two-dimensional delusion of their profile is that you never know what lies beyond their sparkling smile they show off in pictures of them at the beach, on a boat, or at their favorite golf course. After all, his photos might just be the most exciting thing about him. But then of course there is the question that lingers; why is he always traveling by himself?

Then there are rare occasions when you meet someone in (gasp) person. He made you laugh, he was charming, and you left the date feeling intrigued. But you just couldn't wait for the next date, so you decided to perform a harmless Internet search. Let's be real:

Some people are just not very photogenic. Suddenly you're questioning the real connection you had because even though your first impression of him was solid, your date with his social media profile left you unsure if you are "meant to be."

When it comes to dating it helps to unplug in order to connect. If you are using someone's profile to even decide whether or not to ask them out, then you fooling yourself and possibly letting a terrific partner go to someone else. Let's not forget what a real relationship is. It is one in which you have human interaction with one another and not to be in some pretend relationship with some *self proclaimed prince* in another country. Social media and dating only go hand and hand if you are actually dating and if you are seeing each other in real life. And a relationship is only a relationship if you are actually in one.

Recently I wrote a blog post on Sam Darnold, an NFL football player, on this exact topic. NOTE: If you are NOT a couple, you then, therefore do NOT take a couple's picture- together with other couples. People are going to then assume that you are in a relationship even if you don't take said photos in which you are tagged and post them to your IG stories-

Here's a fact about men and social media: Men love to post about "their" woman because they are proud of who they're with- it's an ego thing.

Men also want other men to know – "She's mine, so back off," and keep the other guys in place.

Then there are men, especially athletes, who don't want other women to know that they are exclusive, so they don't post simply because they don't want to leave a trail that they are dating someone to make it easier to hook up with other females. You scare away all potential hook-ups, models, groupies, etc if you post on your timeline that you are in a relationship.

If you follow a lot of athletes on Instagram, you will see that they use the feature of stories very often and very well. They tend to put the girls they are "dating" in those stories and not on their feed. Why? A story only lasts 24 hours and then it disappears. Not everyone will technically see said story of you posing with the girl, so they have a better chance at hiding a romance while at the same time of letting the girl think they are exclusive because they "posted" about them together.

The MAIN excuse you will hear from these guys as to why they don't wish to post on the feed about their relationships are the following: "I want to keep my life private," or, "It's no one's business who I am with and what I am doing." This here is straight up nonsense!

You are already using a social media platform so your life is not private. And you already started posting about other areas in your life, the main areas of your life can't be kept private now. Let me also add that I follow a former NFL player and his wife on Instagram, and one day she posted that she laughs at all the women who end up in her husbands DMS, because they don't know that she reads their private messages... (insert laughing out loud emoji)

A lot of these athletes have public relations people that take over their social media as well, so you really never know WHO is reading their DMS!

There are also people who tend to use social media for the only way they communicate with everyone. If you are dating someone, it would be wise to note that if you have something to say then say it directly to him.

There is also no need to have your business all over social media. I am talking about the feeds on Twitter and Facebook. Even though people may not respond to your nonsense, they will be sitting there reading your wall, waiting for the drama to unfold. And the only person that is left looking like a psycho is you. Social media is not a diary nor is it a laundry basket. Be careful with what you put out there.

Here is a fact: One-third of Americans who use social networking sites use the sites to check up on somebody they once dated. The same is true for nearly half of those ages 18 to 29.

Not only do ex's poke around and spy, but if you are in the process of getting a divorce, chances are your Facebook account has already been looked at by your soon-to-be ex-husband/wife. 90% of divorces today have cited Facebook in their cases.

People using pictures of the opposing party that involve teenagers drinking alcohol served by a parent to a pictures of a husband at a nightclub dancing

with a babysitter. You name it, and it's been used in a divorce case. That is why it is crucial to be wary of what you post because what you post can ALWAYS come back to bite you in the booty!

Remember it's not the actual social media that ruins relationships. People who don't respect relationship boundaries do. A cigarette and embrace after sex has quickly been replaced with a scroll through social media. Men and women are guilty of reaching for their phone and basking in the glow of their screen rather than the afterglow of lovemaking. (as said by a sex therapist)

The easiest rule I have is this one: Use real-world boundaries on social media. Imagine that your social media behavior is happening in person. Would you make that comment or send that message with your partner watching? If you wouldn't do it in the real world, don't do it online.

With social media and dating, comes the world of snooping and the feelings of jealousy that social media bring to any relationship. If you feel the need to snoop on your partner's social media pages then there's a bigger conversation that you need to have about your lack of trust in the relationship, or your feelings of insecurity. I have heard of couples sharing passwords and stuff, but is that really necessary? If you don't trust them right off the bat, then why are you with them in the first place?

Social media is important for many reasons these days, business wise and personal. But when we get into a relationship we need to make sure that we have the social media converation.

Here are a three things that can either make or break a relationsip thanks to social media:

1) If your ex from three years ago can make it a point to creepily watch every single one of your Instagram stories like clockwork, then it goes without saying that your current partner should be doing the same.
2) Special occasions like birthdays, anniversaries and Valentine's Day are definitely days to acknowledge. And a nice way for you to see that they're proud of your relationship.
3) Go through each other's social media timelines together and show off who you are friendly with in real life and who on line are your "online friends" - be open about what you do on line right off the bat, this saves face later on.

Have you ever noticed that you mostly see happy faces in pictures, and stories about success?

Seeing happy mothers displaying happiness while catching fun with their kids doesn't indicate she's happy. She may be suffering from depression.

You shouldn't be surprised at the same time seeing two lovebirds flaunting each other on social media.

One of the parties may be suffering from domestic violence. Seeing people putting on a smiling face can be deceptive when it comes to social media without you knowing what the relationship looks like in reality. The idea that the relationship is "perfect," can be from from it.

Social media is a place where you can meet some really great people and some really creepy ones all in the same day! You can create online friendships and business parnters, just as you can create a love story from time to time. But, remember that people you have met online are still strangers, no matter how long you have been talking to them or how friendly they are.   So, how can you know who to trust and who you can't trust?

He or she must respect you in all aspects, meaning that the person knows the limitations of your relationship. A few of the big no-no's are: stalking you in all social media profiles, harassing you with spam messages, or asking you for very personal information. A major red flags to look out for is if someone you meet on Facebook, Instagram, Twitter or any otehr playfirm starts to ask you for money. Then there is a good chance that he or she is not trustworthy and just looking to scam you. (We will get into this later on in the book.)

Remember, those who choose to hide behind their blue screens are not to be trusted! Even video calls are not enough to say that you completely trust the person. Face-to-face interactions are significant in every relationship, even online ones have to meet every now and then. If they keep refusing to meet up with you, that should be a clear cut sign that they should not be trusted and that they are keeping information from you.

The whole point of making friends online is to find people who you relate to that can enrich your life; not people who add stress to it.

In closing, remember that social media doesn't ruin relationships, not respecting someone's boundaries is the cause for why relationships break up using social media. Social media can put negative pressure on friendships, especially when one friend is very active about posting pictures, status updates and opinions that hurt others. People also need to remember that, social media can make it much harder to have meaningful connections or bonding moments when you're doing it virtually. Social media has certainly shifted the way we communicate and relate to the world around us. In some ways, we are able to remain connected to friends who are far away or whom we do not get to see regularly in person, and this is great. However, it's important to note that while sending memes back and forth allows for continued contact, investing in friendships on a deeper level is an important part of maintaining positive relationships.

Human connection requires that we invest more deeply than that. We can become so seduced by the ease of connecting with others online that we begin to think that these relationships are more intense, more committed and more complete than they really are. We run the risk of alienating the people who populate our daily lives in pursuit of intimacy with our online friends. We each have only so much intimacy to go around, and we need to make sure we're investing it for our own maximal benefit.

The lifestyles you are scrolling through may change how satisfied you are in your relationship because they seem to be better than what you have. A 2013 study found that, among couples who had been together for less than three years, spending more time on social media was linked with more social media -related conflict and more negative relationship outcomes.
One study found that those who are dating people who overshare tend to have lower relationship satisfaction (though positive posts about the relationship itself every now and then seemed to mediate that effect).

Now, as I have stated before, it's important to have each member of the relationship publicly post that they are together, it's another to go ahead and overshare and over post. There are certain information that should be kept private, your address/phone number and email being the most obvious.

With your medical information and traveling schedule a close second.

Also, I don't want to know that your boyfriend/husband is a jerk, and that she is cheating on you. Remember, it's not a laundry basket, it's social media . Just because we are behind screens, it doesn't mean that you should treat people any differently than if you were to be in front of them.

Social media can be a great way of communication, but as you can see, it also has its pitfalls. Therefore before you spend hours on social media, rather try to have real-life conversations with your friends and loved ones. And if you are looking for a list of places to meet people in person, rather than online, here's your "cheat sheet" to do just this.

Bars, restaurants, coffee shops.
Church
Volunteer – Charities or coaching youth sports
Sporting Events
Malls and grocery stores
Gyms
At the dog park
Parks in general
Libraries
At a friend's party

Chapter 4: Dating And Violence (off line as well as online)

When you hear the phrase, abusive relationship, usually domestic violence comes to mind, but emotional abuse is often minimized, yet it can leave deep and lasting scars. There are three types of emotional abuse that most don't even recognize as abuse. They are:

1) Verbal abuse: yelling at you, insulting you or swearing at you.
2) 2) Rejection: Constantly rejecting your thoughts, ideas and opinions.
3) Gaslighting: making you doubt your own feelings and thoughts, and even your sanity, by manipulating the truth.

Verbal Abuse

An emotional abuser's goal is to undermine another person's feelings of self-worth and independence. Emotional abuse falls under the category of domestic violence but it's always overlooked since it's not physical. Emotional abuse may be accompanied by other kinds of abuse: being sexual, financial, or physical. However, it doesn't need to include other kinds of abuse to count as abuse. We all get into arguments from time to time. Sometimes we lose our cool and yell. It's all part of being human. But verbal abuse isn't normal.

First, let's look at what a normal disagreement won't look like to give you some context as to what verbal abuse is and looks like.

A normal disagreement won't dissolve into name-calling or personal attacks and they don't happen every Arguments usually revolve around a basic issue. They aren't character assassinations as you listen and try to understand the other's position, even when you're angry. During a normal conversation, one of you may yell or say something truly awful out of frustration, but it's an unusual occurrence and you work through it together. Finally, even if you can't agree completely, you're able to compromise or move on without punishments or threats.

Remember, you have the right to feel safe, respected and supported in your relationships.

Here are some of the red flags that should signal to you that you could be in an emotionally abusive relationship.
1) They insult or attempt to humiliate you. Then they accuse you of being overly sensitive or say that it was a joke and you have no sense of humor.
　　2) They frequently yell or scream at you and arguments take you by surprise, but you get blamed for starting them
　　3) The initial disagreement sets off a string of accusations and dredging up of unrelated issues to put you on the defense. They try to make you feel guilty and position themselves as the victim.

4) They save their hurtful behaviors for when you're alone but act completely different when others are around.

5) They get into your personal space or block you from moving away. They hit the wall, pound their fists, or throw things. They want credit for not having hit you.

Rejection

Rejection can be experienced on a large scale or in small ways in everyday life. While rejection is typically a part of life, some types of rejection may be more difficult to cope with than others. In the field of mental health care, rejection most frequently refers to the feelings of shame, sadness, or grief people feel when they are not accepted by others. In romantic relationships, rejection can be in many different forms. The most typical form is achieved by communicating to a person that he/she is useless or inferior and by devaluing that person's thoughts and feelings.

Rejection includes the following behaviors:

1) Displays of rejecting behavior toward someone, often [purposefully or unconsciously] letting them know, in a variety of ways, that he/she is unwanted.

2) Putting down someone's worth, or belittling their needs. Calling someone names or telling them that he/she is worthless.

3) Making someone a scapegoat and blaming someone else for their problems.

4) Refusing to talk to someone and giving them the "silent treatment."

Gaslighting

Gaslighting is a form of psychological abuse where a person or group makes someone question their sanity, perception of reality, or memories. People experiencing gaslighting often feel confused, anxious, and unable to trust themselves.

The term gaslighting derives from the 1938 play and 1944 film "Gaslight," in which a husband manipulates his wife into thinking she has a mental illness by dimming their gas-fueled lights and telling her she is hallucinating.

Gaslighting often develops gradually, making it difficult for a person to detect. According to the National Domestic Abuse Hotline, techniques a person may use to gaslight someone include:

Countering: This describes a person questioning someone's memories. They may say things such as, "you never remember things accurately," or "are you sure? You have a bad memory."

Withholding: When someone withholds, they refuse to engage in a conversation. A person using this technique may pretend not to understand someone so that they do not have to respond to them. For example, they might say, "I do not know what you are talking about," or "you are just trying to confuse me."

Trivializing: This occurs when a person belittles or disregards the other person's feelings. They may accuse them of being too sensitive or of overreacting when they have valid concerns and feelings.

Denial: Denial involves a person pretending to forget events or how they occurred. They may deny having said or done something or accuse someone of making things up.

Diverting: With this technique, a person changes the focus of a discussion and questions the other person's credibility instead. For example, they might say, "that is just another crazy idea you got from your friends."

Stereotyping: An article in the American Socializing Review states that a person using gaslighting techniques may intentionally use negative stereotypes of a person's gender, race, ethnicity, sexuality, nationality, or age to manipulate them. For example, they may tell a female that people will think she is irrational or crazy if she seeks help for abuse.

While anyone can experience gas lighting, it is especially common in intimate relationships and in social interactions where there is an imbalance of power. A person who is on the receiving end of this behavior is experiencing abuse. (Source: American Socializing Review and National Domestic Abuse Hotline)

Now that we discussed verbal abuse, here are also 3 different types of abuse that happen in relationships: 1) Domestic Violence 2) Rape and 3) Dating abuse.

Let's tackle the first one: domestic violence.

DOMESTIC VIOLENCE

Earlier in the book I mentioned Abuse isn't always obvious and I gave you some red flags that everyone reading this should know and note.

It is estimated that 960,000 incidents of violence against a current or former spouse, boyfriend, or girlfriend, compared to 3 million women, are physically abused by their husband or boyfriend per year. Women ages 20-24 are at the greatest risk of nonfatal intimate partner violence.   Every 9 seconds in the US a woman is assaulted or beaten. Domestic violence is the leading cause of injury to women—more than car accidents, muggings, and rapes combined. Domestic violence victims lose nearly 8 million days of paid work per year in the US alone—the equivalent of 32,000 full-time jobs. And the most stunning statistic is: Men who as children witnessed their parents' domestic violence were twice as likely to abuse their own wives than sons of nonviolent parents.

[Domestic Violence Resource Center and Domestic Violence Statistics]

This is why we need to put an end to abuse, because it is a cycle that just continues and continues. Recognizing the warning signs can actually save someone's life. If you suspect that someone you know is being abused, speak up! Telling yourself that it's none of your business, is one of the main excuses as to why nobody tries to interfere. But keep in mind, most times people are afraid to come forward and speak up about this since they feel ashamed, embarrassed, or helpless.

Abusers are very good at controlling and manipulating their victims. They have such lack of respect for human life but they also have very low self-esteem. That is one of the reason they are abusive.

Just like bullies on the playground, people with a lack of self-esteem often terrorize someone who has self-esteem. Jealousy is often one of the other reasons why the bully picks on a person. The bully gets self-esteem through terrorizing his/her victim. They make this person somehow eventually believe that they are worthless, incompetent, and rejected. Not only is it a power trip for the bully but they are also gaining negative self-esteem by taking away your positive self-esteem. And to most people, this is the hardest relationship to leave.

10 Warning Signs that someone is experiencing domestic violence:

1)Tries to control you by being very bossy or demanding.

2) Is violent and / or loses his or her temper quickly.

3)Tries to isolate you by demanding you cut off social contacts and friendships.

4)Pressures you sexually, demands sexual activities you are not comfortable with.

5)Makes "jokes" that shame, humiliate, demean or

embarrass you, whether privately or around family and friends.

6)You frequently worry about how he or she will react to things you say or do

7)Abuses drugs or alcohol.

8)Is jealous or possessive toward you.

9)Your family and friends have warned you about the person or told you that they are concerned for your safety or emotional well being.

10)Your partner "rages" when they feel hurt, shame, fear or loss of control.

If you can relate to at least 3 of these behaviors, you are being abused and you need to get out now before you get dragged further and further into the relationship. So the next logical question is: How do you get out of an abusive relationship?

First, make sure you're safe. Speak with a trusted adult. If the person has physically attacked you, don't wait to get medical attention or to call the police, do so immediately. Assault is illegal, and so is rape — even if it's done by someone you are dating.

Second, don't rely on yourself alone to get out of the situation. Friends and family who love and care about you can help you break away. Many times, people in abusive relationships isolate themselves from family and friends. This is not the time to feel ashamed asking for help. Those that care about you, want to see you happy. They will be more than willing to aid you in anyway they can.

Third, you can look up a list crisis centers, teen help lines, and abuse hotlines on Facebook and Google. These organizations have professionally trained staff to listen, understand, and help.

Fourth, it takes as much courage to stand up for yourself in any given situation. Everyone has an equal right to happiness. No one has a right to take that happiness away from you. The first step is definitely the hardest: making that important decision to leave. Making that decision is tough but it is empowering. And remember, there is no place for abusive in LOVE.

RAPE

The U.S. Bureau of Justice Statistics states that 91% of rape victims are female and 9% are male, and 99% of rapists are male, using the definition of rape as penetration by the perpetrator.

The Department of Justice released this definition of rape on it's website since I wrote, "Hello Love, Where's Cupid?"

Definition: The penetration, no matter how slight, of the vagina or anus with any body part or object, or oral penetration by a sex organ of another person, without the consent of the victim."

U.S. Justice Department's Bureau of Justice Statistics, found nearly 250,000 rapes or sexual assaults occurred in 2011, when I first wrote, "Hello Love, Where's Cupid" and in 2019, the number doubled to 406,970 women who were raped or sexually assaulted.

1 out of every 6 American women has been the victim of an attempted or completed rape in her lifetime. Among all victims, about nine out of ten are female.

Ages 12-34 are the highest risk years for rape and sexual assault. Those age 65 and older are 92% less likely than 12-24 year old to be a victim of rape or sexual assault, and 83% less likely than 25-49 year old. Young women are especially at risk. 82% of all juvenile victims are female. 90% of adult rape victims are female. Females ages 16-19 are 4 times more likely than the general population to be victims of rape, attempted rape, or sexual assault. Women ages 18-24 who are college students are 3 times more likely than women in general to experience sexual violence. Females of the same age who are not enrolled in college are 4 times more likely.

Sexual assault is one of the most under-reported crimes, with an average of 39% being reported to the police each year.

The closer the relationship between the female victim and the offender, the greater the likelihood that the incident will not be reported.

When the offender was a friend or acquaintance, an average of 71% were not reported.

42% of rapists are never married.

Every 2 minutes, someone in the U.S. is sexually assaulted.

Time of day sexual assaults occur:

- 43% between 6:00pm and midnight.
- 33% between 6:00am and 6:00pm
- 24% between midnight and 6:00am

- Nearly 6 out of 10 sexual assault incidents were reported by victims to have occurred in their own home or at the home of a friend, relative, or neighbor.

The average age of an arrested rapist is 31 years old.

Why would someone who experienced sexual assault wait years to come forward?

Research shows the answer is complicated.

The public may not realize just how many victims of any crime blame themselves for their own victimization. Self-blame is one of the most toxic forms of emotional abuse. It amplifies our perceived inadequacies, whether real or imagined, and paralyzes us before we can even begin to move forward. Seemingly innocent questions from family and friends can trigger self-doubt and prevent victims from reporting to police.

They may also question what they did wrong and believe it was their fault. Sexual harassment and assault can be a humiliating experience to recount privately, let alone publicly. Victims of sexual harassment and sexual assault in adulthood or sexual abuse in childhood tend to feel shame, because as human beings, we want to believe that we have control over what happens to us. When that personal power is challenged by a victimization of any kind, we feel humiliated.

Another reason women don't go to the police is that they fear of the repercussions when it comes to reporting sexual harassment or assault — fear of losing their job, fear they won't find another job, fear they will be passed over for a promotion, fear of losing their credibility, fear of being branded a troublemaker, fear of being blackballed in their industry, fear of their physical safety, etc. The fact that sexual misconduct is the most under-reported crime is due to a common belief that women make up these stories for attention or to get back at a man who rejected them. Victims' accounts are often scrutinized to the point of exhaustion.

Also women feel it is useless to come forward, because they have seen the way others have been treated. They feel it is hopeless, because they won't be believed, and their reputations will be tainted, if not ruined. Women who have already been sexually assaulted or harassed feel especially helpless, since the chances are extremely high that they did not receive the justice they so desperately needed.

To all the men out there focusing so much energy on trying to figure out why victims don't report, it would be far more productive to ask, "Why do we allow men to continue to sexually harass and assault women?"

Survivors of sexual assault are:

   3 times more likely to suffer from depression
   6 times more likely to suffer from post-traumatic stress disorder
   13 times more likely to abuse alcohol
   26 times more likely to abuse drugs
   4 times more likely to contemplate suicide

   [Source: Rape Crisis Center]

How to protect yourself from being raped

The old advice was to watch what you wear, how you act, and what you say. But, why should a woman have to change her behavior to protect herself?
So, here are some real tips on how to protect yourself.

Body alarms are devices that when pulled, trigger a loud piercing sound which attracts attention to you. For information on these contact your local police department. Physically resisting makes sense if you are certain the rapist is unarmed and if you think it won't make him angrier. If you think that your natural reaction would be to fight, make sure you are aware of an attacker's vulnerable body areas such as the groin, eyes and Adam's Apple. Take a self-defense course!
Use anything that may help you escape, but consider that any weapon you use may be taken by the rapist and used against you. Use only what is easily available. Some examples are: combs, keys, pins, hairspray, or various other aerosol sprays.
Guns are another means of self-protection, but they are very dangerous. Statistics show that it is more likely that a gun will be used against you than to protect you against an attack. If you do decide to carry a handgun, it is absolutely necessary for you to license it and learn how to use it correctly. It could mean your life.

Disgust your assailant by claiming you have a sexually transmitted disease (STD) or your period; urinate, fake a convulsion, even vomit. Screaming may work if you are in a populated area. Yelling "Fire" is also an effective strategy designed to get help from strangers.

Another idea is to stall if you don't believe that you can escape. Buy time with any method that may cause the assailant to let his guard down. Engaging him in conversation or pretending you are ill may prove effective. Stay calm!

If you are out at a bar or club, NEVER leave a drink unattended. If you do, ditch it and get a new one. Also, never accept drinks from strange men ... thank them, but don't drink it.

DATING ABUSE

Nearly 1.5 million high school students nationwide experience physical abuse from a dating partner in a single year.
One in three adolescents in the U.S. is a victim of physical, sexual, emotional or verbal abuse from a dating partner, a figure that far exceeds rates of other types of youth violence.
Approximately 70% of college students say they have been sexually coerced.

Girls and young women between the ages of 16 and 24 experience the highest rate of intimate partner violence -- almost triple the national average.

About 72% of eighth and ninth graders are "dating".

Only 33% of teens who were in a violent relationship ever told anyone about the abuse.

Research presented at the American Psychological Association convention in Honolulu showed that about one in three U.S. teens ages 14 to 20 have been victims of dating violence, and about the same amount say they've committed relationship violence themselves- both boys and girls! Here are the rest of the findings: Among girls, 41% reported being victims and 35% reported committing dating violence themselves. Among boys, 37% said they had been victims, and 29% admitted to being perpetrators. Girls were more likely to have committed physical violence, but more likely to have been victims of sexual violence. Meanwhile, boys were more likely to report committing sexual violence.

[Source: American Psychological Association]

Teens and young adults experience the same types of abuse in relationships as adults. This can include:

- **Physical Abuse:**Any intentional use of physical force with the intent to cause fear or injury, like hitting, shoving, biting, strangling, kicking or using a weapon.
- **Verbal or Emotional Abuse:**Non-physical behaviors such as threats, insults, constant

monitoring, humiliation, intimidation, isolation or stalking.

- **Sexual Abuse:**Any action that impacts a person's ability to control their sexual activity or the circumstances in which sexual activity occurs, including rape, coercion or restricting access to birth control.
- **Digital Abuse:**Use of technologies and/or social media networking to intimidate, harass or threaten a current or ex-dating partner. This could include demanding passwords, checking cell phones, cyber bullying, sexting, excessive or threatening texts or stalking on Facebook or other social media. [Source: Love is Respect]

Dating violence often starts with emotional abuse, as mentioned in the beginning of this chapter.

Some other things to note:
** Teenage girls in physically abusive relationships are much more likely than other girls to become pregnant. Abuse can get worse during pregnancy, and it can harm the baby growing inside you. Never get pregnant hoping that it will stop the abuse. **

When it comes to preventing teen dating violence, the ultimate goal is to stop the violence before it even begins.

As a result, the most effective prevention begins by educating preteens and young teens about how to form healthy relationships with others. It also involves teaching them important life skills like assertiveness and solid communication skills. They also should learn how to disagree with others in a healthy and respectful way.

The most common warning signs are displaying jealousy, asking for passwords to one's devices or accounts, and insisting on spending every free moment together.
As your kids grow, look for opportunities for them to practice sharing their thoughts and feelings. And when you can, empower them to say no to things they do not want to do.

Let's STOP it before it STARTS.

(Source: Very Well Family)

Chapter 5: Myths: sexual myths, Out of My League Myths, How To Get a Guy To Chase You and Other Myths.

If you just went on a date, wait three days before texting or calling. Men don't like when women ask them on a date. When you're interested in someone, it's best to play games and have them guess your feelings instead of being upfront.

There are lots of "rules" out there about love and relationships. If you dig into the science behind dating and romance, you'll learn that many of these rules are based on complete misconceptions. I'll start with the myth of some guy/gal is "out of your league."

Dating today has made it easier than ever to find and list data points that quantify, and place value on, our romantic prospects. A little LinkedIn sleuthing clears up questions about wealth and education; Facebook and Instagram fill in the looks and social status gaps. And somewhere in the cauldron with all that is a "league." Dating based on a league system is making a judgment call as to how it stacks up against your own, and using the result to inform the way you treat others who might be interested in you. Put that way, it's clear: It's rude. The whole thing is classless, narcissistic and shallow. Despite what model agencies, magazines, dating apps and the rest of the world would tell you, there is no Top-

Tier League of people. You are the keeper of your own value and your own worth.

Have you ever crushed on someone that you never even considered asking out or flirting with because you thought there was no chance they'd say yes? Go ahead, raise your hand, you know that I am talking about you!

When we say "out of someone's league," often we're talking simply about looks, but sometimes it's a combination of attractiveness, wealth, social status, and other assets. The idea is that one person is distinctly and recognizably "above" another person in these ways, so of course they wouldn't date them.

I've come to believe that the "out of someone's league" concept traps us in thought patterns that are both harmful and false. When we do this, we're saying that certain people, with the sum of all their qualities that we really don't know yet, by assumption, are objectively worse or better than others – and more or less worthy of romantic love.

When we rank people like this, we're ignoring a basic truth: People want different things in their romantic partners. It's ridiculous to think that we can reduce all those different qualities into a single universal ranking of "leagues." Which again, it just utterly rude and obnoxious.

Men often say, "She's out of my league," but what these guys are actually doing is creating an imaginary system of worthiness in dating, and then deciding that's the only basis on which a woman should be allowed to choose a dating partner.

Never mind chemistry or personal tastes. If she's within his league, based solely on her adherence to socially constructed beauty ideals, then she should be willing to date him. If she's not, then she's a stuck-up bitch who thinks she's too good for him. You know, her "standards" are too high.

Ranking women in "leagues" is a way for men to avoid thinking of women as individuals with unique needs, interests, and desires.

The concept of "out of my league" was created by a guy who didn't want his confident friend to go out with a girl HE had HIS eyes on, or felt was attractive, so he INSISTED that she was "out of his league" so this way, he didn't pursue her.

It's classic jealousy.

It's also RIDICULOUS to think that guys will LISTEN to other guys when they ask the dumb question, "Do you think I have a shot with her?" Basing happiness on what OTHERS think is not only harmful but wrong. You are the one who lives with all the decisions you make, your friends and family don't.

In life, it's a given that some people will like you and some people will not. I've seen so many examples of couples who are "mismatched." That is—those couples who seem to be ill-paired because one of them is so much better looking than the other. When I stop to think about it, it really does make this notion of a "league" laughable.

Science tells us, as I did point it out in "Hello Love, Where's Cupid?" that if we spend more time together that we are more likely to become attracted to one another. Your own concept of who is in your league can be heavily skewed, and if someone's interested, you shouldn't worry about them being out of your league.

I would by lying if I said the media doesn't impact our standards, because it certainly does, but those unrealistic standards that the media sets are not definitive. It is for that reason — *that standards are personal constructs and not completely social constructs* — that leagues don't really exist. The line, 'he/she is out of my league' is simply an individual's way of mind-fucking themselves into backing out of possible rejection. But we are all looking for different characteristics in a significant other, it's impossible to label one characteristic better than another. This is another reason why someone is never "out of your league"

Instead of creating low-self esteem and focusing on your flaws as a reason why a specific man or woman doesn't want to date you, look at your flaws through an empowering new lens. Whatever the flaw, own it and transform it into a prominent feature. Nothing else can transform your self-confidence so quickly.

So in the craziest time of 2020, 2021, it's time to retire this nonsense dating myth called Out Of My League. No one is out of anyone's league. Dating is all about self-confidence, self-worth, and finding a partner who not only builds you up, but someone who holds you down when times are tough.

There's no "sports" league for that.

Another dating myth that I have seen a lot of people posting videos about on TikTok is "How to get a guy to chase you." I realized there are dating coaches and dating books that actually tell you that this is a strategy. Well, it's not surprising.. But that doesn't make it an effective advice. I'm here to tell you that "making men chase" often backfires and is a myth that keeps on living.

Let him chase because that's what men want. They are hunters at heart. hey like chasing the prey. This is all you hear. Well, it MAY work for SOME guys, But the truth is the "let him chase" advice is that it doesn't work with the best men. It works with boys.

The best men are are busy, and have their goals, dating options, and are socially active. By socially active I mean that they are out in the social scene and don't need an App to "help" them get women. Also, in this day in age, there is one theory that folks with the "let him chase you" concept forget: men chase very little -if at all- when there is an abundance of women. When women are scarce, the culture tends to become highly romanticized. Men pursue, chase and engage in ostentatious displays to woo women.

(Source: Date-Onomics)

Yes, if you show that you're confident and you don't 'need' somebody, you appear like you've got lots of options and so you must be a good catch. The problem is, that if you pretend that you're really not into having someone there for you, you're going to be an attractive choice for a guy that's not that into commitment, just as you are portraying.

If you are playing games, all you are doing is showing others that you are insecure, and you are setting yourself up again for heartbreak. By playing hard to get, you could be fueling someone's desire to win. As soon as they "get" you, they'll soon realize they didn't want you that much to begin with, and you're back where you started.

Also what folks tend to to forget is that there's a difference between liking someone and wanting them. This could explain why playing hard to get doesn't necessarily work. Yes, the chase is fun, no doubt, but then what happens when you get what you wanted? To most, they stop doing all the little things that they did to get the person's attention. They stop putting that person first. Basically, they stop doing everything they did to win you over and you get to then see who them for who they really are.

Note, that if someone you like is not responsive to your messages, texts, calls, etc, this doesn't necessarily mean that they are playing hard to get. Instead, you should take it for what it is — a lack of proper communication, or simple rudeness. Don't bother chasing them.

Another dating myth is making him wait for sex.

To sleep with him or not to sleep with him isn't really the question...date 3 or date 6 is beside the point.

It's based on the theory that men want quick sex and women want relationships. When you give quick sex, most experts say, men get what they want and have less interest in sticking around. When there are more women than men, the culture devolves into more of a hookup culture. (like today!)

Today men and women are viewed as more similar, that men aren't ready, prepared and willing to do the long-courtship thing.

Even men looking for relationships tend to end up with women who help him along the dating process.

The most successful women focus on going through each level of the relationship together instead of "getting as much as possible" while giving as little as possible.

That means that <u>when good quality women are abundant, waiting games are more likely to backfire</u>.

I see men graciously wait every day. Women aren't the only ones who want to know if this is going somewhere. Men who are relationship-ready want to know that you're taking them seriously too. And if you're quick to hit the sack he'll wonder if that's your pace with *every* man.

A grownup real man who is looking for a relationship will let you know when it's time to move into the next phase of the relationship. There will be no guessing, period. Relationship-minded, grownup men are not into playing games. They just want to meet a nice woman, have an easy time getting to know her and eventually end up with one wonderful partner to share the rest of a great life. Now, there are guys out there that say that the it is the girl/woman that decides whether or not sex is going to happen and that he "instantly" knows on the date if she is going to decide to sleep with him.

That's part of the myth too. See, every relationship is different. You can't go by what every book says, what every so called expert says, and what every magazine article tells you. The belief that people are more worthy of marriage if they wait X number of dates than people who don't wait that number of dates is a misogynistic attempt at controlling people's bodies.

This means that there's no timeline that you should be following for things like:

- holding hands
- kissing
- spending the night

"What's most important is that you and your partner are all enthusiastically consenting and ready. You shouldn't have sex, she says, if or when:

- you feel pressured to have it

- you feel it's your only option or your only way out of the situation

- you feel that you owe it to another person

The last dating myth I will discuss is always a fun one: Men should be the ones to doing the asking: IN other words, women can't ask men out.

There is no rule book when it comes to dating.

If you don't ask, you don't get. We are in the year 2021, and for some stupid reason there is still a lot of pressure for women who are interested in men to *wait* to be asked. And although there are *some* straight men out there who don't think women should ask men out, there's data that suggests that the majority of straight men would be into a woman asking them out— it just doesn't happen that often.

This is because you hear dumb guys in the media and experts say, "*Women asking men* on first *dates can* be taken as aggressive, desperate, and masculine. At the very least, it *can* signify a loss of power."

No offense to these guys, but shut the fuck up! That's an attractive quality: A *woman* who *will ask* for something she wants, not just expects. If *women* start *asking guys out* on *dates*, it'll become a more normal way of doing things, and all of these fears *will* become eradicated.

Of course sometimes it's not so easy to make a move if you've grown up being told that dudes will seek you out if you exude interest and work a come hither look, but in 2021, it's time to break free of these sexist ideas when it comes to dating.

Asking guys out is the best way to weed out the creeps. If a dude is weirded out by me being assertive right off the bat, I definitely don't want to be dating him or sleeping with him. I used to be pretty awkward about it but I think I've gotten better. You're talking to another human here, not a transcendent alien man being. Talk to guys just like you'd talk to anyone else. Rejection is only scary if you take it too personally.

I make it short and to the point. It doesn't have to be super sexy or romantic. Don't make it weird and it won't be weird. Plus, asking guys out is about owning my sexual power. I don't wait around for life to happen to me, and I don't wait around for someone to ask me out. Besides, most of the time they're totally taken aback and it's cute.

Oh, and as for me, I only want to be one guy at a time. The idea of dating as many as possible at the same time is stupid. It's also not the point of a relationship. The point is to be exclusive with each other.

However you feel about making the first dating move, know that thousands of women have come before you and totally nailed it — and/or failed miserably, but lived to tell the tale.

Chapter 6: The 5 Selfish Traits

This may sound funny but it's true.

People who are selfish don't know they're being selfish.

They just assume they're nice people who care about their own happiness more than anything else. In the dating world and social media world of today, there are more narcissist people/selfish people than ever before!

Why?

That's a great question.

A relationship with a selfish person means that they take your love without giving back in return. They think that they are needed more than they need you. For them is is take, take, take. Unfortunately, the traits of selfish people are not easy to notice. Most of the time, they are people pleasers and hide their dark side very well. Here are the 7 traits that they exhibit. We will go through 1 at time. Most of these you will notice that athletes and celebrities have, as well as folks in high-powered positions.

1- They do not show weakness or vulnerability.

2- They don"t accept constructive criticism.

3- They believe they deserve everything.

4- They do not listen to those who do not agree with them.

5- They criticize others behind their backs.

They do not show weakness or vulnerability.

He or she will ignore the fact that everyone has weaknesses, but them. Selfish people see being vulnerable as a weakness and therefore, hate to show it. Vulnerability is not winning or losing; it's having the courage to show up and be seen when we have no control over the outcome. Vulnerability is not weakness; it's our greatest measure of courage. From an early age boys are often taught by parents, unconsciously and sometimes explicitly, to hide their feelings. It's how the 'big boys don't cry' mantra develops and can be perpetuated by teachers, friends, society and the main stream media. In some ways we are getting better at teaching emotional acceptance to boys/men.

But back into the dating world, most men/boys don't like to show their feelings or the fact that they are feeling vulnerable.

I get it. When you first start to date someone and are really into them, yet at the same time you're still unsure if they're the right person. What if they hurt me? What if they cheat? What if they don't feel the same way? What if they're not who they say they are? All those feelings are accurate and understandable. No one wants to waste their time, feelings and energy on someone who is just using you or doesn't feel the same way. Fear shows vulnerability. Why would we want to be vulnerable and put ourselves out there when we can just happily keep doing whatever it is that we are doing and be perfectly just fine. It's comfortable, right?

Let's go back to that person you have been dating and starting to get those feels for. Why not let them know how you feel? Why not get to know them more, take that leap, and see if it's worth it? If you never ask, the answer will always be no. Deep down, we all would love to find that special someone who we can share our life with. What's the worse that could happen? They don't feel the same? Great, now you don't have to waste your time and can open yourself up to other prospects.
But that would be how a "normal" person would feel and handle a situation like this stated. When it comes to a selfish and narcissist person, they handle this situation all wrong!
The ego of a selfish person will not allow for vulnerability. They will never commit to something or someone unless they are getting some sort of benefit from it. And most of us don't realize this until we are knee-deep into a relationship with them.

They don"t accept constructive criticism.

People who display a selfish attitude, believe others will attempt to devalue their work and their potential. Therefore, they will try at all costs to not recognize constructive criticism, often defending themselves which is ironic.
People's ego doesn't allow them to accept that they are wrong.

Selfish people are characterized by inconsistency when pursuing their goals.

In other words, selfish people believe they deserve EVERYTHING! They believe that they will always be successful because they just are, not caring who they have to get out of the way in order to get what they want and not caring what they have to do in order to get it as well. They are not only self-centered but also have a false sense of entitlement. A manipulative person refers to someone who seeks to control people and circumstances just to achieve what they want. They might use emotional blackmail. These people are skilled manipulators by instinct and a control freak at heart. Selfish people are manipulative and they're looking to get something out of you for their own benefit.

They do not listen to those who do not agree with them.

When you say something to a selfish person, even if it's constructive, hey will think that you are their enemy and you do not deserve their respect or attention.
Criticism is good because it lets you learn from the opinions of others. But a selfish person has no time to broaden one's horizons and grow.

Humility is a precious human virtue that we need in order to grow as people and as social beings in our environment. Egocentric individuals will only cover up this personal potential, looking for ways to stand out and amplify their achievements.

Selfish people criticize others behind their backs

Selfish people prefer easy judgment and nothing is easier than judging behind a person's back. Be warned: A person content to sit with you and criticize others will speak critically of you as well. Why do selfish people do this on a regular basis?

<u>Pride</u>

They see the faults in others, but not themselves
The judge others, saying it loudly, so that others see the faults of others, and not their own.

<u>The are extremely judgmental</u>

They just enjoy talking about others and pointing out their imperfections to others because it makes them look better and stronger. They like causing trouble by "getting all the dogs barking" and then enjoy watching the trouble they created.

<u>They often very envious, jealous and small minded</u>

They don't like it that others admire people who are bigger and better than themselves

<u>Displaying their immaturity</u>

They could well be deceivers who hide the truth about themselves which show that they are not as genuine as others believe they are and they should not be trusted.

No matter how great we are, there is always someone who is not satisfied with it and there is always someone pointing fingers at you. Here are 6 simple things to do when people talk behind your back

1) **Why are they doing it?**

It's not rare that we find ourselves cornered in life. Be it in school, college, family or work place. It's not the easiest of things to deal with when the ones you trusted are bitching about you behind your back. And *the worst part of it all is you hardly ever know the reason*. It could all be a huge misunderstanding or a misinterpretation of what you said or did. And sometimes simply because your actions hurt somebody without your knowledge.

2) **What others think of you is none of your business!**

If it is just somebody in your friends circle or family or at work place you are not too close to, here is a quote I read a while ago: *"what others think of you is none of your business"*. It's best to ignore them and carry on with life. Try not to get affected by it. Block it out of you mind and stay calm and say it's not your business and laugh it off.

3) **If it is someone who matters to you**

If it is somebody that matters to you, nothing better than sorting out with them. Talk it out! It works most of the times between close friends and family! Remember, be prepared to hear unpleasant things. Cause, yes, they're pissed off for some reason. They'll throw muck at you. Just stay calm and take it. *Tolerate!*

4) **Give it some time**

Hear what they have to say. And give it some time, think before you tell them how you feel. See if it was reasonable for them to have done what they did. *If they were right and you were insensitive, accept it and apologize.* There's nothing shameful in accepting a mistake. It won't make you a smaller person. If things work out, you'll end up feeling like a bigger person when things are sorted out.

5) **Tell them how it made you feel**

Let them know how it made you feel as patiently as you can. It's very natural to get emotional when you're talking with somebody so close to you about something that's so personal. *Prepare, if necessary rehearse* what you are going to say to them before you go and talk to them. That way you can make sure you emotions don't affect your conversation. You gotta think straight :). You screw it up here, it might never be the same again.

6) **Before All this – Ask yourself – Is it really worth it?**

It's got to make sense now! If it doesn't, it's not worth fighting with such people. It's not easy to just let somebody put you down. Don't take it if you think the person is not worth it. But you won't know who is worth it and who isn't until you try.

So try talking it out with them and if doesn't work out, remember the first rule, *you don't have to waste your time and energy thinking about what worthless people think about you!* But trying to sort it will save you from regretting it later. You'll have the satisfaction that you did your bit to clear the problem. And if it doesn't work, you will at least look like the bigger person, which to a selfish person is the best revenge of all.

Remember, social media is FILLED with rumors, gossip and lies. Social media and dating apps are both filled with the perception that everyone's life is perfect, that everyone is successful all the time and that everyone is flawless.

When it comes to the social media/ dating apps vs. reality: it's all about perspective.

Let's get this argument about which is better — a per-social media or a post-social media society — out of the way and admit I can't answer this question

Yes, it was better for our eyes when we weren't spending so much time in front of screens. But technology has also brought us a level of productivity and education never before realized in the history of the world. But, for anyone that has spent any amount of time scrolling through social media, it is no secret that it can foster a sense of discontentment, insecurity, or even depression. When we see others accomplishing more than us, it can breed low self-esteem or even a lack of self-worth.

And when we use dating apps and have people reject us for being ourselves, it can cause us to become bitter, insecure and feel completely worthless.

Among other dangers that social media/dating apps might possibly pose in our lives, such as lack of privacy, is this habit of always comparing ourselves to others.

People, when they are happy, post a lot of happy things. But when I'm not happy I will consciously, or unconsciously, compare myself to others. As a result, I create a world that is not a true world because I imagine that everybody is happy in that world, except me .

 If we perceive that everyone else is perfect, then we push ourselves to become someone that we are not, and then we get frustrated, and then we get depressed.

If you go to a bar, and you notice a guy, and you think he's hot, and you're looking at him, and he kind of ignores you, it's one rejection. But with dating apps, you see dozens of people, and you only "match" with those people whose profiles you like who also like you. If you never match with the people you like, "it can feel like continuous rejection. Folks that will perceive themselves as being rejected are far more likely to feel anxious or depressed when they're on these apps. Allowing all external websites with complete strangers to decide your value is a mistake.

And when you are online you are surrounded by selfish people. People who troll you looking to break you. People who troll you looking to mess with your mind.

People who troll you looking to make you feel that your worth is determined by how they look at you.

Stop letting "these people" win and start giving yourself permission to succeed at life and love -with your own terms.

Chapter 7: Red Flags

This chapter really explains itself. There are tons of red flags before you date someone seriously. Here is that list.

1- Still talks to their ex/ has them on social media.
2- Takes hours to repply to you
3-According to him, all his exs are "crazy"
4- When he is in the car and his bluetooth is hooked up and his guy friend is calling and he starts the conversation with, " Hey John, say hi to Jane she's here with me," This is code for don't talk about any of his side chicks.
5- When he says the following either in person, on the app or in a text:
- I can't commit to a day I can see you.
-Hey sexy.
-I'm still living with my ex, but we're just friends.
-I'm just super busy right now.
-Women never message me first. Change my mind.
-Don't hate me if I'm funnier than you.
-Swipe right if you're down to go with the flow.
-My friend made this for me.
-1am – you up?
-What's your snapchat?
-I don't like to talk on the phone
-Drinks at my place?
-They only compliment your body
-They only talk about themselves

-They leave you on read during the day and only answer you at night.

-He follows tons of girls that are half naked or dressed in their biknis

-He only wants to hang out at night and in private

-They constantly tell you how perfect you are.

-They have a hard time saying they are sorry.

-They are always critizing you

-They have rarely been single- always in a relationship

-He is a little "too" private

-He posts stuff about his life on social media but NEVER posts about being in a relationship with you. (IG stories don't count!)

-He brags about his chivalry

-He calls himself a Mama's boy

- He's a self-proclaimed "old-fashioned type of guy."

-He makes a point of frequently showering you with gifts

-He says I love you on the 2nd date

- He talks a lot about what a nice guy he is

-He wants you to spend every second of every day with him.

-They never compromise

-They don't want to label the relationship as you're their "girlfriend" and they only tell folks that they are "seeing someone"

-All they want to do is hang out and have sex

-They are never proud of your accomplishments

Now, let's talk about the Red Flags in Women:

-She tells you that she doesn't like to talk about her past
-She constantly shows clevage when she is out and in all her social media posts
-She uses sex to get what she wants from you
-She expects you to pay for EVERYTHING all the time
-She becomes batshit crazy and takes everything out on you. Then instantly becomes Ms. Nice and acts like she just didn't throw all the plates onto the floor
-She is constantly jealous of you and of every female you talk to and demands you only talk to other guys
-She doesn't trust you and asks to see your phone
-Constantly accuse or suspect you of cheating
-Constantly calls and texts you and becomes angered if you don't immediately respond
- Want to know a play-by-play of everything you do
-She literally just broke up with someone and started dating you immediately
-All her Exs were jerks
-She's rude to others in public
-She Shows Signs of Serious Substance Abuse Issues
-She talks bad about her friends constantly
-She is clingly and needs to be with you 24/7
-She shops A LOT .. like everyday and spends money she doesn't have all the time.
-She pretends to be stupid
-She never posts about you on her social media and when she does, she has to always be in the picture.
-She's cold-hearted when it comes to others

-She never wants to introduce you to her family

-She is a party girl and has to go out every night

-Bathroom Selfies

-She has hobbies

-She makes fun of your dreams and constantly belittles you

-She doesn't have any "girl" friends they are all male

-She calls herself a Princess

-She can't commit to anything.

-She is superficial

-She flirts with guys in front of you to see how you will "react"

Red flags are just that, "red flags" but the main thing to listen to when it comes to dating someone, is your intution. Your gut feeling about someone is always, always, always right. When I was younger I failed to listen to it so many times and had to pay the price of having to deal with heart-wrenching heartbreak.

Your intuition is a very real psychological process where the brain uses past experiences and cues from the self and the environment to make a decision. The human brain has two 'operating systems'. The first is quick, instinctual and effortless. This is where our intuition lies. Intuition works by drawing on patterns collected by our experience and when we have to make a quick decision about whether something is real, fake, feels good, feels bad, right or wrong, etc.

So the best advice I can give to you on intution is to do the following:

1- Feel
You'll feel it in your mind and there will be goosebumps your skin, send a shiver down your spine, race your heart and quicken your breath. Sometimes it's even more subtle and the only way to describe it as a 'knowing'

2- Shh... just sit still and listen
Your intuition can't talk to you if you're not listening. When you start to take notice, good things will happen.

3- Trust
Ever notice that sometimes we get "sick to our stomach" when we need to make a decision or are worried about something? That is your intution at work.

If something doesn't "feel" right, then it probably isn't.

Chapter 8: Lies, Scams and One Night Stands

Dating sites are good at baiting people to try them out. They lie about how many active members they truly have, use fake profiles, get you to take out your wallet by having guys or gals message you or show interest. But, remember, just because it is popular, doesn't mean it actually works!

I believe online dating has made single women overall less happy, less likely to find a long-term partner, and more at risk of sexual violence.

Here are reasons why you should stay away from these sites all together.

Tdid you know that the Federal Trade Commission sued online dating service Match Group, Inc. (Match), the owner of Match.com, Tinder, OKCupid, PlentyOfFish, and other dating sites, alleging that the company used fake love interest advertisements to trick hundreds of thousands of consumers into purchasing paid subscriptions on Match.com.

The agency also alleges that Match has unfairly exposed consumers to the risk of fraud and engaged in other allegedly deceptive and unfair practices. For instance, the FTC alleges Match offered false promises of "guarantees," failed to provide services to consumers who unsuccessfully disputed charges, and made it difficult for users to cancel their subscriptions.

They believe that Match.com conned people into paying for subscriptions via messages the company knew were from scammers. Online dating services obviously shouldn't be using romance scammers as a way to fatten their bottom line.

Match allows users to create Match.com profiles free of charge, but prohibits users from responding to messages without upgrading to a paid subscription. According to the FTC complaint, Match sent emails to non subscribers stating that someone had expressed an interest in that consumer. Specifically, when non subscribers with free accounts received likes, favorites, emails, and instant messages on Match.com, they also received emailed ads from Match encouraging them to subscribe to Match.com to view the identity of the sender and the content of the communication.

The FTC alleges that millions of contacts that generated Match's "You caught his eye" notices came from accounts the company had already flagged as likely to be fraudulent. By contrast, Match prevented existing subscribers from receiving email communications from a suspected fraudulent account.

Many consumers purchased subscriptions because of these deceptive ads, hoping to meet a real user who might be "the one."

Not only has Match been sued, but Online dating services, including Match.com, often are used to find and contact potential romance scam victims. Fraudsters create fake profiles, establish trusting relationships, and then trick consumers into giving or loaning them money. Just last year, romance scams ranked number one on the FTC's list of total reported losses to fraud. The Commission's Consumer Sentinel complaint database received more than 21,000 reports about romance scams in 2018.

What do actual people who used Match think about the site? Here are a few folks "reviews"

Ruth:

I paid for a month's subscription ($34) and as soon as they got the money they started sending me creeps as potential partners. I couldn't see likes (I paid for it) and everything I was supposed to get as an upgraded dater was not given. They lied. Also there is absolutely no way to get in touch with them (even though they have contact us on their page) to complain about anything. My advice to anyone who is contemplating paying money... don't waste it!!! It's not worth it.

Jen:

I had issues with males soliciting for sex and Match did not even respond. The people I were matched to were NOTHING like my preferences. Match is no different than guys hiding behind profiles in order to lure you to their place to have sex, once! Then ignore you and tell the women after you that you are a stalker, as they will be labeled when their one night of sex is over. Don't pay to be on this site, ever!

Joann:

Although, I've heard mixed reviews for Match.com, sadly, this particular site is terrible. They quickly take your money and, if you seek a refund within the same month (I signed up the beginning of January, 2021) --- they indicate it should have asked "within the first 3 days"! The majority, if not all, the profiles are not real. I would like a complete refund for the 6-month subscription so I'm not forced to report fraud.

Charles:

Site is full of fake profiles. Many fake likes and conversations. You can tell the conversation isn't real. Answers given either don't make sense or are intentionally vague and provide zero depth and go nowhere. If you are discerning about your potential match, I would avoid match.com. Not saying there isn't romance to be had on there, but it's not even close to the way commercials represent this site. Better off trying to meet people IRL

The next dating site that is popular and that you probably have seen the commercials is Eharmony. Eharmony launched in the United States in 2000 with its patented Compatibility Matching System® which allows eharmony members to be matched with compatible persons with whom they are likely to enjoy a long-term relationship. There is NO scientific algorithm to "meet people" based on what Eharmony is telling you. Simply put: It is a bunch of shit that they are selling you.

Here are what people who have used Eharmony truly think of the service.

Jessica:

I am a female matching with males. Psychology professor Barry Schwartz found that having an infinite number of choices is detrimental, paralyzing and exhausting. There are many profiles with zero pictures. Many that will message for a day or two and then disappear. I don't know if it's eHarmony bots or real men with Choice Overload. Whereas I have 3 matches in my city and one has no picture. One has no eyebrows. And one hasn't read my message yet. It doesn't seem like anyone on is there in my age range for a committed relationship.

Courtney:

After using their service for 6 months and spending like 250 dollars I canceled the subscription. There was no match or even a date because all the guys on there were either interested in casual dating or just looking to get laid. Then about 8 month later I get another charge from them for 550 dollars saying I never canceled my subscription and even though I have not used there services in months I will be charged that money. They are the worst company I have ever had to deal with. I am a single mother trying to make ends meet and now I can't pay my bills because that stupid company just stole over 500 dollars from me!

Sally:

EHARMONY ARE CROOKS!!!! DO NOT SIGN UP! I made the mistake over a year ago (Sept 2019) and after 6 months of NOTHING happening, (having paid $377.47 for that waste of time) I wrote to the company and told them their "system" was not working for me. Their "promise" of free months if not successful never happened. I CANCELLED my account and never heard another thing from the company.......until I was billed $287 in Sept 2020! I immediately contacted the company and told them I had canceled my account and had not corresponded with anyone since. No emails from the company, etc. I was told I must log into my account. I responded that I could not, as I had canceled my account six months prior. They told me I had not canceled my billing auto renewal therefore I owed the annual fee. I have called several times and told customer service I used the services only 6 months with NO SUCCESS. Customer service were never helpful. Not when I was trying their service, not when it didn't work and I voiced my concern, therefore I canceled; not when I canceled my account and not when I called to clarify I had canceled my account after they charged me. eHarmony does not care. They just want your money. What a rip off!!

Pauline:

After paying well over $300 for a years' subscription eHarmony has not provided one single person that I would be interested in meeting. I have opened my search up to the entire North American continent and still not one single man has revealed himself. I thought maybe Covid is keeping people off the site. Now I think eharmony just doesn't have the membership that other sites have. I would not recommend eHarmony to anyone unless you want to waste your money. My membership will not expire until the end of this year. Big deal. I thought time would help but now I doubt it. I feel like a marooned single woman on a deserted island.

Tammy:

I wouldn't even give it one star. Worst site ever. They charge you a TON of money and want to offer you packages that are a year or two long. First, most people I know including myself aren't trying to be on this site or any dating site any longer than they have to. So only offering an ungodly high monthly package, their only other options are 1 or 2 year plans which are still really high! Again who is trying to be on a dating site for that long! Ridiculous. Then when I finally did sign up there are almost never any new matches, it's the same people all the time!

** Tammy hit the nail on the head:
  1) You aren't trying to stay on a dating site for 1-2 years if your goal is to meet someone to date exclusively and then hopefully marry.

2) The dating sites are not in it for your happiness-
   they are in it to make money off you by getting
   you to sign up long term, not send you actual
   matches, not have you meet quality people, etc.
   The goal for them is to tug your heart strings and
   have you pay them for as long as possible!

Of course then, there's Tinder. The one site that has
brought on more STD's, more unrealisitic relationships,
and most important, the site that most athletes use to
find their one night stands when on the road.

Here are some of the reviews from more actual users
and what they had to say to me, will shock you.

Mark:
Tinder has been engaging in bait and switch tactics for
years in which Tinder will send " bait" to lure me to
purchase thousands of dollars of add ons called "super
likes" then allow them to either disappear without use,
be used on an overwhelming number of bot profiles or
obvious fake profiles so that the consumer has to re
purchase / replenish the super likes in order to get the
few that actually do as they are advertised. I have
undoubtedly spent thousands of dollars on these add ons
and the bait switch program is alive and well at Tinder. If
you are on the website long enough it becomes readily
obvious that they engage in this practice by design. So
why stick around? Because inevitably you'll make a few
contacts on the site that become important to you so you
are essentially "hooked" or "bound" by the relationships

you've built. Tinder knows this and uses it as bait to further lure you into purchasing more super likes.

Jon:

Tinder is an absolute joke of a dating site. 98% of the profiles are either fake, girls just looking to be Instagram stars, or they live 5000 miles away from you in another country. The ones that are real, if you do happen to match with them, never respond after a few back and forth messages. When you first sign up for tinder, you seem to match with half of the girls on there which make you think the site is great. you send all of them a message, you never receive a response. Just a bunch of fake profiles. You would have to be a fool to pay for tinder. Not sure why they ask for your city and distance. You are willing to travel for dating, the profiles that come up are girls that live overseas. Tinder should be shut down.

Peter:

In the present climate of (COVID 19), we are surrounded by, we may be looking to find that special someone. So if you have 90+ matches on Tinder... it might be a matter of time before you find that special connection. Well I have found... nothing, no help from the actual site, no matches that I had come across in the few times I have had to view. As we all have a busy life planning for a better future mostly. Bottom line I think or feel, based on my own personal experience. My quality time has been wasted on this site. I still haven't met a match despite having more than 90 matches.

Tony:

I had an account for years and never met any females. They are all scammers or pros, all expecting to be paid. No one really looking for a relationship. I got tired of all the posts asking for $s or gifts from Amazon and responded once with a smart ** answer. For that I was banned for life with no opportunity to appeal, there is NO way to get help!!! Don't waste your time or $s!!!

Caroline:

Started using Tinder this year. I would say up to 95% of the men on here are either married, engaged, living common law or in some form of a so called "committed" relationship. The few single men on there are also only looking for hook ups. A lot of online dating site junkies who are on at least 3 other sites are predators on Tinder too. How do I know? Easy, some junkies are so obsessed with being online that it doesn't take long to figure out they're also chatting with your single friends who are on other sites!! I dated one guy only to find he was begging a close friend who was on POF, of to go out with him too. He had no idea. If you want to find a nonsleazy relationship, stay away from Tinder. I'm sure there have been some success stories but I can't imagine it's that many.

The next popular site is Bumble.

Bumble works a little differently. On Bumble, if you're a man searching for women, all you can do is like her profile. It's then up to the women to decide how far things go by responding or not. Even if a connection is made, men can only send a single free icebreaker and extend the connection another day.

That though, doesn't stop the complaints.

Jennifer:

I signed up for Bumble dating after hearing the company has had a record amount of financial success. The CEO just became the youngest self made billionaire. I liked the idea that this dating app is different because it's female led - Men aren't allowed to send the first message. And then the matching process began...just with photos of potential men. No background. I don't know anything about them. The site said, "Great! We have an idea of what your type is!" The hell you do! Good matches are not just about looks. Currently there is no background check service available either. If you're going to on-line date, a critical step you have to do is look up potential dates through their county clerk of court site. All you need is their full name. It's free. Keep yourself safe because this site is not going to do that for you.

Cathy:

Bumble suggests that Premium will enable you to see more men who are interested in you. I took the bait and I just got to view more blurry, overweight guys holding fish. They say Premium allows you to establish more detailed preferences, but when you do set your preferences, the app quickly run out of possible matches and continues suggesting you revisit profiles you've already swiped left on. The alternative, the app suggests, is to revisit and edit your preferences. Endless loop of failure. As well, there are tons of fraudulent accounts. Enormous time and energy on setting and resetting preferences with no results. My request for a refund after one week of trying Bumble Premium was denied.

Mike:

Many of the people who contacted me were fake. Some of the profiles I rejected were sent multiple times. I know that they are fake! There are so many fake accounts on the site that it is not worth responding to anyone. Customer service did not address my concerns, so I am posting them here. The company plans going public next year. LOL Investing in this company?? You must be kidding me. Stay away.

Paul:

I've tried Bumble for some reason. I guess it sounded a little better than other apps. After using it for a bit it just felt like other dating apps which try to get you to sign up. Using it made me feel like I was ugly, worthless, and like I was supposed to be alone. If I would get a match the timer would run out. I got the impression these were taken accounts trying to get you to pay money and just preying on lonely people.

Lee:

Hundred and hundreds of fake profiles. Foolish site that lures you in because they want to sell your photos for facial recognition. Reported underage girls, and Bumble took too long to take action. They say women must write first. What a joke. You'll never get more than a Hi. Closed account with this waste of time site.

I could seriously go on and tell you what some folks told me about Cupid, PlentyofFish and so forth, but I believe this here has made the point that dating apps are a BUSINESS they are NOT for any other purpose than that.

I don't care if you best friend from Phiilly, met her husband on here ten years ago, or Trisha from Texas fell in love with Tom on one of them, etc.

Remember, we want to believe that true love is out there. Secretly everyone including the toughess SOB you know wants to be swept off their feet in love, romantically, unconventionally, and spontaneously. But that does not happen using social media nor using dating apps.

Recently I was reading comments people made about how sex is used today as weapon to lure someone in.

The comment was this: "Sex used to be about enticing people. Luring them in, flirting, building up. Now every single person I talk to tries to talk to me about how "dominant" they are in bed or what their kinks are within the first lines of conversation. I mean.. I'm a woman talking to men and I just do not understand- what you guys are thinking? I'm so tired of sex being treated like a contract. It's boring, it's not exciting. Like my GOD does anyone have a bloody personality?"

And here's the thing that we all forget. The ideal dating partner would be physically attractive to the person pursuing them while also having a cultivated, humble personality. Unfortunately, if they're the type of person who's attractive to EVERYBODY (or thinks they are), it rarely shakes out that way. People are only interested in the quick and easy hook up because dating apps have made it easier without a doubt and no one has to put in the work to have a relationship when you have many places on your device where you can get "nooky."

You can rarely form a natural connection through a screen - especially when most communication is done over texting. It gives people too many perceived "options", such that they treat people like objects. It easily allows people to develop warped perceptions about the other person (for example, if you are a girl with a few glamorous photos they may perceive you as someone who is very open about sex and offend you asking about your kinks etc) and hide a lot of important things about themselves. Body language is so important for forming connection and this is lost with online dating. You could speak to someone for months over messaging and think you know them, when truly you don't know someone until you've been in their company for an extended period of time in multiple different settings and occasions. Most people are talking to multiple people at once so nobody trusts each other. There's no natural community of mutual friends and gradual getting to know each other through innocent low-pressure interactions and events, that helps you to feel comfortable in each others company. Everything is either too rushed and pressured or is way too extended through chatting online that neither party is really enjoying that much.

A new study, done by Love Connection, compiled data from dating apps, law firms, and numerous other studies to figure out how the pandemic affected couples across the country in 2020. It seems many haven't been handling it very well.

According to the study, couples' intimacy suffered throughout the past year as 50% of partners reported a decline in their sex life, while 27% even said they felt a decrease in relationship satisfaction. However, 46% said they had not really noticed any significant changes.

What people don't realize about dating apps in general is that you need a lot of swipes to get a match, a lot of matches to get a number, a lot of numbers to get a date and a lot of dates to get a third date. Trying to find a partner in this way is extremely labor-intensive and can be quite exasperating. This is why folks instead of looking for a relationship, are on these apps for sex. And what has truly happened is that people have grown so used to meeting hookups or partners online that they end up ignoring potential matches elsewhere.

When people are going out, going to a party, to a bar, often they are actually not at all thinking about dating. This means that even if they end up having an interesting conversation with someone they would have swiped right on "it's just not where their brain is" - sad but true. he clarity of a match online has perhaps made us more timid in real life meetings. Without a 'swipe yes' or 'swipe no' function, we risk putting our feelings out there to be rejected in full view. Better to open the app and endlessly swipe, blissfully unaware of who swiped you away. Dating today requires a level of intention that I see a lot of people lacking.

If you're looking for someone that has a professional career, you might want to go downtown at happy hour and make sure that you're talking to people that work in those office buildings, or if you're looking for someone who has a big heart, you go to charity events and places where you're going to meet people who make philanthropy a part of their lifestyle. There is no need to head to your device and think you are going to meet the man or woman of your dreams by simply scrolling through millions of profiles. It is not that easy nor is it realistic.

You may be familiar with the mantra that encourages you to "Say yes" to new things and not hold yourself back. You have to apply that same mantra in your life when it comes to finding love.

You may be surprised to know that many of the places you go every day without even thinking about it are places where you can find potential mates now that the Covid 19 restrictions have somewhat been laxed.

1- Bars

2- Volunteer/Charity Work

3- Book Clubs/ Libraries

4- Sporting events

5-Dog parks, parks in general

6- Gyms

7- Museums

8- Airports

9- Beaches

10- Coffee Shops

11- Grocery Stores

12- Workplaces (although this may not be typical anymore thanks to MeToo!)

13- Weddings and other gatherings

14- Community Events / Fundraisers

15- Street Fairs

16- Professional Networking Groups

17- Music and Art Festivals

18- Colleges

19- Churches / places of worship

20- Cruises

The places to meet people are ENDLESS!

When folks see this they can delete those apps and get back to living life offline. When you focus a life that is not obsessed with social media, dating apps, texting, etc... you will realize just how much you have missed out on.

Your soulmate is out there. And he/she is not on Match, Tinder, Eharmony, Bumble, Ok Cupid, Plenty of Fish, Date Hook up, etc.

They are out there waiting for you to meet them. So the next time you spot someone who catches your eye, try this crazy idea: "Make eye contact and smile!" What happens next may be even more satisfying than swiping right.

Chapter 9: Relationship Impossible

Love just happens.
One minute you could be at a grocery store, a coffee
shop, or even at work minding your own business
and BAM- cupid's arrow strikes you. You find yourself
feeling flushed, having sweaty palms, and you
are tongue-tied all because you laid eyes on someone or
bumped into them. You can't explain how or why got
"that feeling" but all you know is that you want to see
that person again.
That what they call, "the unexpected." You didn't plan on
it happening, set it up to happen that way, or went out of
your way for it to happen, it just did.

I'm not into this "games playing" like some girls out
there are today. And if you watch enough Tiktok videos,
that is what these "socila media dating experts" are
telling girls to do- play love games. I will though let guys
know a little secret: We know that you guys spy on us on
social media. We are always one step ahead of you by
posting pictures of ourselves either alone or with friends
when we look amazing. We know how to play the game,
and getting you jealous or curious about us, is how we
do it. We aren't as "stupid" as you claim us to be. But
the amount of time we spend on our phones trying to
"bait" each other on social media, is what is ruining
relationships and making them completely impossible.

If you've ever felt like you're competing with your partner's phone for their attention, you're not alone. The time we dedicate to our screens can change how we approach our partners in real life.

When we're constantly tied to our phones scrolling through Instagram, reading the news, or checking emails, we have to learn to balance this time with being offline. It's especially important to ensure we don't forget about our loved ones in favor of screen time. It is almost impossible to create or enhance relationships when social media is, in the first place, taking our time and attention away from who is in front of us. Social media can have a positive effect in our lives, but social media can negatively affect relationships when you start comparing yourself to other people, including your friends, just based on their social media accounts. For example, some may fear their lives aren't as good as their friends' and withdraw from friendships because they feel they're not good enough. If you're constantly comparing your life to a picture-perfect image that others put forth on social media, you might not feel good about yourself, and you may be more likely to develop depression. Building healthy relationships is founded on being yourself, not trying to be someone you're not, or hiding parts of yourself, as we often see on social media day in and day out.

A Pew Research Center survey conducted in October 2019 finds that many Americans encounter some tech-related struggles with their significant others.

For instance, among partnered adults in the U.S. – that is, those who are married, cohabiting or in a committed relationship, roughly half (51%) say their partner is often or sometimes distracted by their cellphone while they are trying to have a conversation with them, and four-in-ten say they are at least sometimes bothered by the amount of time their partner spends on their mobile device.

Partnered adults under the age of 50 are particularly likely to express the feeling that their partner is distracted by their phone, with those ages 30 to 49 most likely to report this. Fully 62% of 30- to 49-year-old and 52% of 18-to 29-year-old who are in a romantic relationship say their partner is at least sometimes distracted by their phone when they're trying to talk them. Still, this issue is not confined to younger age groups: 41% of partnered Americans ages 50 and older say they have encountered this in their relationship at least sometimes.

With phones being such a distraction, people might be tempted to look through their partner's phone. However, there is widespread agreement among the public that digital snooping in couples is unacceptable. Seven-in-ten Americans – regardless of whether they are in a relationship – say it is rarely or never acceptable for someone to look through their partner's cellphone without that person's knowledge.

Still, 34% of partnered adults say they have looked through their partner's cellphone without that person's knowledge, with women being more likely than men to say they have done this (42% vs. 25%)

For many adults, social media plays a role in the way they navigate and share information about their romantic relationships. Roughly eight-in-ten social media users (81%) report that they at least sometimes see others posting about their relationships, including 46% who say this happens often, but few say that seeing these posts affects how they feel about their own love life.

Moreover, social media has become a place where some users discuss relationships and investigate old ones. Roughly half of social media users (53%) say they have used these platforms to check up on someone they used to date or be in a relationship with, while 28% say they have used social media to share or discuss things about their relationship or dating life. For adult users under the age of 30, those shares who have used social media to checked-up on a former partner (70%) or posted about their own love life (48%) are even higher.

But social media can also be a source of annoyance and conflict for some couples. Among those whose partner uses social media, 23% say they have felt jealous or unsure of their relationship because of the way their current partner interacts with others on these sites, and this share rises to 34% among those ages 18 to 29.

Still, some users view these platforms as an important venue for showing love and affection. This is especially true for younger users who are partnered: 48% of 18- to 29-year-old social media users say social media is very or somewhat important for them in showing how much they care about their partner.

At the time of the survey, four-in-ten Americans who are married, living with a partner or who are in a committed relationship say they are often or sometimes bothered by the amount of time their partner spends on their cellphone, including 12% who say they feel this way often.

In addition, 24% of partnered Americans report that they are at least sometimes bothered by the amount of time their partner spends on social media, while a somewhat smaller share (15%) say they feel this way about their partner playing video games.

There are certain groups who are more likely to express annoyance over their partner's digital activities than others. Among partnered adults, women are more likely than men to say they are often bothered by the amount of time their partner spends on their cellphone (16% vs. 8%) or playing video games (7% vs. 3%)

Beyond gender differences, people's attitudes also vary by age. Some 18% of partnered adults ages 18 to 49 say they are often bothered by the amount of time their partner spends on their phone, compared with 6% of those ages 50 and older. Younger adults in romantic relationships also are more likely than their older counterparts to say they are often bothered by the amount of time their partner spends on social media (11% vs. 4%) and playing video games (7% vs. 3%).

When asked to reflect on their partner's cellphone use, 51% of Americans in a romantic relationship say their partner is at least sometimes distracted by their cellphone when they are trying to have a conversation with them, including 16% who say their significant other is often distracted by their mobile device.

Women who are in a relationship are more likely than men to say their partner is often distracted by their phone while they are trying to hold a conversation, but this gender difference is most pronounced among younger adults. Three-in-ten partnered women ages 18 to 29 say their significant other is often distracted by their phone while they are trying to hold a conversation, compared with 15% of men in this age group who say this.

Americans – regardless of whether they are in a relationship – were asked in the survey about their views about some issues related to technology and relationships. For example, they weighed in on the acceptability of looking through a significant other's phone without that person's knowledge.

Seven-in-ten U.S. adults say it is rarely (28%) or never (42%) acceptable to look through a significant other's cellphone without their knowledge. Smaller shares – about three-in-ten (29%) – view this behavior as at least sometimes acceptable.

Majorities across major demographic groups view these actions as unacceptable, but there are some Americans who are more accepting of this behavior than others. Women are more likely than men to think it is at least sometimes acceptable for someone to look through their partner's cellphone without their knowledge (35% vs. 24%). And about one-third of adults under the age of 65 (33%) view this as acceptable, compared with 16% of those 65 and older.

Americans' views on the acceptability of looking through a partner's phone varies by current relationship status. Americans who are married or cohabiting are more likely than those who are single or in a committed relationship to say that looking through a significant other's phone without that person's knowledge is sometimes or always acceptable.

And there are many apps that allow you to basically snoop on ANYONE you want at ANYTIME.

For Instagram, there is a website that allows you watch Instagram stories without the person knowing.
This site is named: https://storiesig.com/

You can also check out any private account on Instagram using https://www.iglookup.com/ Now, I don't recommend using them, but they work. The reason I am telling you all this is simply to know, that what you post is being viewed even if you don't think it is. There are many people who use these tools to see what you are up too. BE CAREFUL of what you post. If you have to be "private" about what you are posting, then that is the cue to NOT post it.

There are also ways to spy on someone using spy apps for the cell phone. Now, there are MANY but there are 5 good ones. If you want to know what they are, then read chapter 10.

But there is a trend that I spoke about briefly called "Ghosting" - which I like to still call "spying," because in reality that is what is it.

I think people who do this might *sometimes* realize they're missing the person they've backed away from, but, they're not willing to admit it. It's also one of the tactics commonly used by Narcissists who 'always want you to go to them' - they rarely concede to make the effort to come to you - which should alert you to the unhealthy balance of the relationship you might have begun with such a person. What they do is to get to know you, but hold you at arm's length; They may say/do everything they can think of to "soften you up" and make you like them & want to spend time with them - then they vanish and you hear nothing. This is their way of trying to emotionally manipulate you into being curious about them or wanting to be with them. Some who 'monitors your Profile' might be very literally "keeping an eye" on you because, even though they haven't expressed their feelings towards you, they don't want to see anyone else getting close to you.

"Orbiters" sounds like an appropriate term to describe such behavior, perhaps night hawks might be another, even though it's used in metal detecting. I don't tend to think it's innocent casual "curiosity" that causes people to do this, I think it's an element of control freak in their personality. Ghosting is directly associated with how uncomfortable people are willing to feel. Social media spying isn't new but it done way more than people think it is. The term should be 'a ghost sighting'- they're gone, but they still linger. But today, there's a difference between "Ghosting" and "Orbiting."
Orbiting is the term used now when someone is spying on you on social media.
Why do folks do this type of stuff? For one, humans are naturally curious, and are well known gossipers. We want to know what's going on. Hormones can bind us to past partners, despite our logical brain knowing what happened is gone and will no longer return Hope is another very human characteristic. No matter how

hopeless things may seem, there is the fantasy that the future will be different. Love is transcendent. The heart remembers. Some people though, are pathologically crazy! And take things a step to far.

Is orbiting stalking? Does orbiting progress to stalking?

Let's dig deep into stalking for a moment.

First, when talking about social media we are talking about cyberstalking. Cyberstalking is the use of the internet, or other electronic means to stalk, or harass, an individual, group, or organization. It may include false accusations, defamation, slander and libel. It may also include monitoring, identity theft, threats, vandalism, solicitation for sex, or gathering information that may be used to threaten, embarrass or harass.

Cyberstalking is a bit different than physically stalking an individual, but it still can get scary.

Some folks take the spying of a person online too serious and start to send direct messages to folks where they make threats, outlandish statements or bully another. Those people who spy on their prey and then have contact with that individual, now have moved into the stalking phase. This person isn't acting like a fan of yours, more like someone who is jealous, has anger issues, and is trolling you to get a reaction of yours. Now if this person does somehow stalk you in person, you need to act quick to resolve it.

Being physically stalked is something that I am sadly familiar with because in college it happened to me.

Back in college I was stalked by this guy. I had completely NO interest in him whatsoever. He liked to hang around a friend of mine back then. First he got my friend to give him my number. Then he invited himself to my house. He called my house. He spoke to my parents. He constantly bothered me. This went on for 2 weeks until I finally spoke up and told him to go away- that I wasn't interested in him at all and I was not friends with him either. (Now, maybe folks know why I am totally against being set up... that's a blog for another day!)

The point being, this could have gone on for months if I didn't stand my ground, send him a clear signal that I was not interested in him at all, not let the pursuing continue. This is why ignoring someone is not the best method to deal with situations. Thinking that they will eventually "go away" is the wrong approach. Remember, you never know what someone's breaking point is, and when you are dealing with emotions, you can't just "let that slide."

Relationships shouldn't be "impossible" but we somehow and for some reason make them that way. For starters, folks need to keep expectations realistic. No one can be everything we might want them to be. Not all differences or difficulties can be resolved. You are different people, and your values, beliefs, habits, and personality may not always be in alignment. Communication goes a long way toward helping you understand each other and address concerns, but some things are deeply rooted and may not change significantly. It is important to figure out for yourself what you can accept, or when a relationship is no longer healthy for you.

Secondly, Conversations quickly turn to arguments when we're invested in hearing our partner admit that we were right or when we are intent on changing their opinion. Choose to approach a conversation as an opportunity to understand your significant other's perspective as opposed to waiting for them to concede. From this perspective, we have an interesting dialogue and prevent a blowout or lingering frustration.

Third, you still have friends and connections outside the relationship and spend time pursuing your own interests and hobbies. You can't spend every minute of every day together. That my friends, isn't love, that is what I call insanity! You need to be able to give someone else space to be themselves. The only way the relationship is going to grow is when you get "me time" away from each other.

An important thing to remember is that relationships are more than about having sex. Communication is the backbone of a healthy relationship, and it's way more important than sex. Knowing that your significant has your back can be more important that getting it while lying on your back. Loyalty, honesty, trust, are all the important factors to look for in another person, not just having a good old romp in the hay.

If you can find that in another person, then that person is going to give you the world. Sex might be easier to get, but true love is harder to find.

Chapter 10: It's all about my Juice

As I was getting this book in order, I had to go back on dating apps. Yikes! So Here are a couple "winners" I found as to what type of guy you find on dating apps, I mean hook up apps, like Tinder:

Bull, 38
Tall. Sane. Clean. Educated. Respectfully dominant and well equipped. Thorough. Verbal, Love role play or fantasy. We only have 1 life to live. (Sounds like someone who is looking for that girl who wants to hook up and just head on over to the bedroom, or hotel room and get some and then it's onto the next.)

Leo, 41
Married dad looking for a submissive to have my way with. (MARRIED... Hello? Do I need say more?)

Hammond, 41

Online dating is so hard when you're a truthful person. I feel like it makes you savage and makes you jaded. Most don't read the profile because all they are looking for is sex and I'm not on here for that. (Sounds like he is trying to sound like he's not interested in hooking up but then why is he even on this app that is all about the hook up?)

Kevin, 34

6'3 = I'm taller than you! I'm not going to remember that I have this app about after 2 months, but message me and I'll get an alert and check it.

Giving this a try because Covid makes it impossible to meet people the old fashion way.

"You look so much cuter with something in your mouth" I hate Nickel back but once in awhile they get it right.
(So, Covid is making it impossible to meet people BUT yet, here he is trying to get a hook up online. Yay! Let's have a-kind-of-hook-up-on-Zoom-or-Facetime!)

Zack, 30

I got a B+ on Human Sexuality in College. So let's just say that I know my way around a *checks poorly scribbled notes*

Clitoris (And Zack's profile picture of him half naked in a pool, where do I sign up? – That's Sarcasm Folks.)

And .... yes, not only do guys have poor choice of words in these bios, but their profile pictures are another thing all together. The sad thing is, women are falling for this crap day in and day out or they wouldn't have that many subscribers to the app.

Craig, 35:

Sometimes I wonder if it's too late for me? Is there even a point to trying anymore? (Seriously, if you clicked on his bio and sent a message you are just as desperate for a relationship as he sounds. Not to mention, he sounds like he needs therapy not a dating app)

Mr Blank, 38

I'm married. Not looking for anything in particular. I'm bored and looking to be entertained. A swipe for me is a swipe for low-self esteem and daddy issues.

(Seriously? I'm so sorry that you are bored in your marriage that your wife is not entertaining you!)

As one guy I interviewed put it, "With these dating apps, he says, "you're always sort of prowling. You could talk to two or three girls at a bar and pick the best one, or you can swipe a couple hundred people a day – the sample size is so much larger. It's setting up two or three Tinder dates a week and, chances are, sleeping with all of them, so you could rack up 100 girls you've slept with in a year." – (and let's add the spread of STD's, other diseases, and yes, unwanted pregnancies.)

If you seriously think about it rock stars and professional athletes have enjoyed easily accessible casual sex for decades. Now with these apps, access to all these women who want to just "do it" makes it one thousand times easier. Tinder allow everyone to seek brief validation in the form of casual sex with a stranger. Why do women, who in the age of "Me Too," want to play the game by the guys rules? What women on Tinder have not realized yet is the fact that men you meet on Tinder most likely are not available; look at the list above, just about all those bios I listed maybe one guy is "available" for a relationship.

Remember ladies, no matter how good you are in the sack, you are not going to turn a casual sex with a guy into a meaningful relationship- EVER.

There are 3 types of women in a guy's mind:

The hook up 2am girl – they would never date or have a long term relationship with her only sex. (These are those girls who are also "good in the sack")

Friend Zone – if you aren't attracted to each other then it's going to be impossible to get out of the friend zone.

Wife material- He sees that you are smart, attractive and he sees that you have a lot to offer.

Do you really think these apps are going to make a guy look for wife material?

If you're looking for a serious relationship, but you allow someone into your life in a "casual way," then that's what you get. If you instead hold out for someone who is also looking for the commitment you are, then you'll get that instead. Behind the scenes, I love judgmental cliches, because they allow me to *instantly* filter out people who think in black and white. Life isn't black and white. It's gray. Here are some profiles that drive me crazy... starting with women:

- Profiles that begin with "I'm divorced."

  So... being divorced describes you in a nutshell? You want a man who has all his ducks in a row, but the first thing about yourself that you want the world to know is that you come from a failed marriage?

  My mom knows Larry Bird's sister-in-law. (Apparently one of the most annoying people ever.) Larry Bird's sister-in-law always introduces herself as "Hi, I'm Larry Bird's sister-in-law," *and then her name.*

FYI Two recent presidents of the United States were raised by single mothers.

Another stupid thing to put in your dating profile:

"You must have a strong relationship with Jesus Christ."

That's cool. Nothing against that. I'm a Christian myself. But if you have such a profound relationship with Jesus, why do you have three children by three different fathers and have never been married once?

How about this one?

" Must be close to your family"

What if *this* is my family? I have got my shit together but they have not. How close should I get?

Another favorite of mine is: "must have shit together"

There are stupid things I see daily on EVERY dating app out there. So here are my top 10:

Stupid Thing #1) **"No drama"** – *Thank Heaven you put that out there; I never would've have known!! Swiping left..*

Stupid Thing #2) **"I'm BAaacckkk!"** – *Thank God you got recycled back into the pool (again): it just wasn't the same here without you! Swiping left, faster...*

Stupid Thing #3) **"I love my kids"** – *Yay, here's your Father of the Year Award and your Mr. Roger's Dad*

Sweater... This is a waste of space: even John Wayne loves his fu*ing kids... next!

Stupid Thing #4) **"Just looking!"** – Newsflash, Dumb-ass: That''s what EVERYONE on these sites are doing!

Stupid Thing #5) "[If you wanna know] **Just ask"**– So, you're a lazy, conversationally empty vacuum that can't put forth any effort. Okay, I'm not shaving my legs, but I'll happily use you for a free dinner... Nope, not even for a good steak with blue cheese crumbles...

Stupid Thing #6) **There are no good women/men left."** - Then why the fuck are you on this dating app knowing full well that these people aren't the "good ones?"

Stupid Thing #7) I'm a **King** looking for my **Queen** or I'm a Queen looking for my King. -Run. Do not walk. Run, from profiles that have this line or some version of this!

Stupid Thing #8) **"Not into weird stuff." - T**his is code for: That's all I am into, is the kinky stuff that you think is weird!

Stupid Thing #9) **"I've been hurt pretty bad..."** Calm down cowboy, we all have. There is this fine line of TMI and casual information and then as soon as dudes cross it on their profile it becomes an instant no-no.

Stupid Thing #10) **"I need someone who can hold a conversation."** This means they can't hold a conversation, and they want you to make up for it.

BONUS:

Stupid Thing #11 "I'm not going to write everything here. You should just message me to really get to know me." - THERE ARE HUNDREDS OF YOU. You HAVE to give me a snippet! I can't message all the hundreds of guys trying to figure out simple things! And then there's so many of them that turn into an angry man-child if you find something that means you're simply NOT compatible!

I seriously don't understand the logic behind this. You are setting yourself up for failure. There's just not enough time in the day

Stupid Thing #12) The one that used to make me want to say...really? Where they mention long walks. I have never liked long walks anywhere... on the beach, shopping, malls or any place else. I don't like the woods or forests or deserted islands either. I don't like desert walks, snow walks or river walks. Walks? Walks to where? And why are we walking?

These are the profiles that keep people binge-watching Netflix... Just say it, you want a man with a big checking account. The only plainer English than that is:

The choice is up to you. Choose wisely.

Talking about long walks on the beach, while at the beach, one summer, I remembered how the weather went from clear and sunny, to cloudy and stormy in a flash. The waves were crashing, the wind was blowing and the lightning was remarkable. Then about two hours later, the clouds vanished, the sun came out shining and the storm was over.

That got me thinking about relationships.

Sometimes a relationship can start out sunny and in a blink of an eye it can get stormy out of the blue.

Sometimes a relationship can be just like the ocean; calm one minute and then stormy the next. Sometimes a relationship can get very stormy and you think it is never going to get better when all of a sudden, the sun comes out, the skies clear, and you feel that the relationship just took a major step forward for the better.

People these days are so quick to end a relationship when times gets stormy. They want the "sunny skies" all the time, but in reality that is just a fantasy. We are human therefore it is normal to disagree, it is normal to fight, and it is even healthy to have arguments from time to time. Not one relationship goes through life without a disagreement from time to time. The movies and TV shows you watch that show how perfect relationships are, are simply fake. The scripts that show a conflict in a relationship and how "easy and quick" it is "fixed," has poisoned our minds. It is a mistake to think that your life can be mirrored from the movies and TV shows you watch.

Ever hear of Cinderella and Prince Charming? Growing up with the fairy tale, that one day a tall, handsome man is going to come riding into town and sweep me off my feet is the reason why many women have an unrealistic view on love. The same could be said about men having unrealistic view on sex thanks to porn. But getting back to how being at the beach has made me think more and more about relationships.

The beach is just like a relationship whereas when you stumble on a seashell that you had no intention of looking for or finding, your excitement for finding that seashell is overwhelming. The same could be said for relationships. When you aren't looking, that is when love finds you. Love is a funny thing, the harder you look to find it, the harder it is to find. But once you stop looking, someone will walk into your life and you'll find it.

I hate seeing girls act desperate for a man these days. They are on dating apps, social media apps, all for the purpose of finding their one true love. They are going about it wrong. They call it falling in love because you just fall. You don't force yourself to trip. Lighthouses don't move around looking for boats. They stay in one place and shine, letting the boats come to them. Just remember that, the person who dances with you in the rain will most likely walk with you in the storm. And that is the best relationship to have and to find.

It's a fact that I owe a great deal of who I am today, to every guy from my past. They have awoken the beast per-say. But because I took a long, hard look at myself, I am able to now be able and ready to love a man who deserves my love and knows my worth. It's not an easy task to look yourself in the mirror, but as I observe many single ladies online and in reality, I have gained insight as to why so many relationships fail.

The first reason is because women have this stupid idea in their heads, that if they don't have a man in their lives they are incomplete.

Dating tip #1: You don't need a man to complete you, you need a man to COMPLIMENT you. There's a distinct difference. To be complete means to love yourself. No man is ever going to complete you and make you whole. You need to complete yourself, by loving yourself.

Dating tip #2: Until a man has actually done something to make you not trust him, don't make him pay for the troubles another man caused. So many times I see people tweeting or posting on Facebook how they don't trust guys, when that guy has done nothing to you to make you feel that he isn't worthy of your trust. Until a man actually lies to your face, cheats on you, or does something to hurt you, don't punish him because the man before him did those things to you! Remember, assumptions ruin relationships.

Dating tip #3: Don't ever feel like you have to chase anyone. Someone who truly appreciates you will walk with you and won't need to be chased. Chasing someone is a complete waste of your time.

Dating tips #4 and #5 go together. There are some guys out there that use love to bait women into having sex with them, and there are women out there that use sex to try to bait men to love them. But what women just don't understand about that "philosophy" is that, dating tip #4: Sex won't make him love you. A guy can love your sex and still not love you. So if you think that he will fall madly in love with you because you are sleeping with him, I hate to break it to you, he's won't. This leads me to dating tip #5: Easy girls open their legs while smart girls open their minds. There's a difference between being classy and being trashy. BE the GIRL that EVERY guy WANTS- NOT the girl that EVERY guy has HAD.

Now to give a tip to the guys out there. And since almost everyone has a smartphone I thought of a great analogy for the modern day man! Dating tip #6: Treat your woman like you treat your smartphone: touch her often, stare at her & make her the most important thing in your life.

Dating tip #7: If the woman is trying to recognize what the man wants in a relationship, she needs to be equally aware of what she wants as well, so she can enter into a balanced relationship, instead of one-sided relationship where she is pleasing and second guessing. When manipulators detect your need to please them, they usually take advantage of your people pleasing weaknesses. That is where the failure comes in, when your need to please a man before you know he is interested in pleasing you, means you're showing signs that some men will exploit.

Relationship means that you expect just as much as you are willing to give. It means that both of you give and contribute to the relationship in different but equal ways because men and woman bring different qualities to the relationship. It means that you both bring the same qualities in terms of love, consideration, kindness, respect, etc. The love is the core of the relationship that keeps acceptance or modification of the differences on track for peacefully resolving issues instead of contention and rejection.

It means that you have a healthy enough self-esteem to know that you should only date a man who shows you that you are [both] valued and respected by showing you he is interested and dedicated to knowing you and what you need.

Dating Tip #8: Men have needs and desires, but they lust for physical pleasure. Relationship in their minds means having a physically rewarding friendship with a woman for a period of time. Men want to have a deeper more meaningful relationship. They need emotional connection without the physical involvement. Learning to have a non physical relationship is important for men.

Dating Tip #9: Most women think they know what a man wants instead of asking him what he wants. Those that ask don't believe him when he tells them what he wants. Then they think they can change him.

You can't change a man.

instead of trying to read his mind on what he wants, ask him and then believe him when he tells you what he wants.

Dating tip #10: There's a difference between giving up and knowing when you've had enough. Don't stay with a partner who isn't giving it their all. So many times people stay with their partner for way too long, hoping that they are going to realize just what you are offering. When the truth is, most times they won't realize what they have and frankly they don't deserve it. Giving up, doesn't mean you don't care. It means that you are tired of giving your everything & ending up with nothing. You know when you have tried to work things out, and if you have done your part and they refuse to do theirs, all you can do is walk away. It's best to be alone and be happy, than to be in a relationship and be miserable!

If you spend too long holding on to the one who treats you like an option, you'll miss finding the one who treats you like a priority. Love comes unexpectedly without any doubt or hesitation. And love should have nothing to do with looks, either.

Back when I was 24 years old, I dated this guy who was a Calvin Klein model off and on for about a year. At first I thought it was pretty neat. But as the year went on I knew that I made a huge mistake. Oh yeah, sure he was what we would call, "hot," but I learned very quickly that looks on the outside are not a mirror to how someone is on the inside. That's why every time I see guys on the internet or hear how much athletes want to date models, I cringe. (Then I roll my eyes)

Our society STILL focuses way too much on a person's outside rather than on a person's inner beauty. Inner beauty, especially to me, is the most important thing I look for in a guy. Yes, that physical spark is needed, but looks are so overrated.

That Calvin Klein model may have been "arm candy" but inside he was colder than ice. (Is that even possible?)

He cared about money, cars, materialistic stuff and but he didn't care about how I felt, what I wanted, he had zero compassion about others, and I was so worried that he wouldn't "love me" based on who I was, that I had to pretend I was someone I wasn't. I can also point out that the other models were just as narcissistic, selfish, greedy, and flat out rude as he was.

It was from this that I learned never to base dating a guy on how he looked but rather than to base it on how he treated me and how he also treated others. A person's personality, their compassion for others, and how they aren't afraid to be themselves as well as not making me feel as if I can't be myself, are the ways I now measure men. Of course, I would be lying if I didn't say that sparks that are driven from physical looks are necessary, but it's not how I make a decision anymore.

It's also important to note that I want to date a man who accept me for who I am, support my dreams as I support his, and build me up to be a better person each and every day. I just don't want to date simply to date. Another reason why so many relationships fail is because so many people do this; they date to just date instead of dating for a relationship. If we date I want you to know that I want to be your second priority. I want your first priority to be you, your ambitions, your dreams, your future, because finding happiness and security alone is critical to finding it together.

Also, we need to stop judging others based on the outer shell of a person. The saying, "Don't judge a book by it's cover," is so true. Why be so shallow? Dating is challenging to begin with, adding extra pressure to yourself and another person is stupid.

Beauty can be intoxicating, but it's also very misleading. And in this Instagram world with so many damn filters, why are we so obsessed with fake and not being real?

Yes, outer attraction matters but in today's crazy world it shouldn't matter that much. Don't get caught up in the Instagram perfection of physical beauty that will quickly fade back once the filters are gone. If you lead with your soul, you're more likely to find yourself in a committed, lasting relationship.

Looks are important in ways that it will get you noticed by someone. In a room full of people our eyes tend to roll on the most attractive people in the room. But then it ends there.

Relationships have a different parameter. It is meant to complete us in ways 'just the looks cannot'.

We may be attracted to someone, initiate the conversation with them, spend quality time with them but we may not necessarily bond with them.

Relationships are just not on the physical level but on spiritual, emotional level where we can connect to the person. Most of the people these days are delusional by the looks. They start their relationship by spotting the hottest man/woman around them. Later when they see their differences they break up. Also personality is a big factor in a relationship. You can be the hottest man/woman in the room, but outside having your looks, be one of the most boring and nasty people on the planet. Here's a secret: What really makes you more attractive than others is your attitude. If we quickly look at a study done published in Personal Relationships it examined the way in which perceptions of physical attractiveness are influenced by personality. The study finds that individuals -- both men and women -- who exhibit positive traits, such as honesty and helpfulness, are perceived as better looking. Those who exhibit negative traits, such as unfairness and rudeness, appear to be less physically attractive to observers. Participants in the study viewed photographs of opposite-sex individuals and rated them for attractiveness before and after being provided with information on personality traits. After personality information was received, participants also rated the desirability of each individual as a friend and as a dating partner. Information on personality was found to significantly alter perceived desirability, showing that cognitive processes and expectations modify judgments of attractiveness.

Perceiving a person as having a desirable personality makes the person more suitable in general as a close relationship partner of any kind. The findings show that a positive personality leads to greater desirability as a friend, which leads to greater desirability as a romantic partner and, ultimately, to being viewed as more physically attractive.

The findings remained consistent regardless of how "attractive" the individual was initially perceived to be, or of the participants' current relationship status or commitment level with a partner.

Previous studies examined physical appearance and personality mainly as independent sources in predicting attraction. By presenting this information in installments, the study simulates a more typical context in which seeing the person's appearance precedes learning about their personality, and shows that perceptions of a person's physical attractiveness may change over time due to their positive or negative traits.

This research provides a more positive alternative by reminding people that personality goes a long way toward determining your attractiveness; it can even change people's impressions of how good looking you are.

Here is something that most don't know:

Mere exposure to someone repeatedly increases the likelihood we will be attracted to them. his is backed up by 50 years worth of scientific research that has found that proximity is one of the most powerful indicators of attraction. We simply are drawn to the people we see frequently.

Over the years, people have said that it is a fluke when two people share a special bond called chemistry. People have said it's not real, but if you know someone in a relationship that has lasted longer than any of those Hollywood relationships, then obviously it's real.

To have *true* chemistry, two people MUST meet the following criteria:

1- It <u>cannot</u> be a one sided attraction.

2- It <u>cannot</u> be forced.

3- There <u>must</u> be a sexual connection pulling the two together, although the connection goes deeper than just feeling something sexual.

Regardless of your definition of chemistry, it is a feeling that is sent from our brains that tells us that we have a connection to someone and that we need to be with them no matter what it takes. [Think Romeo and Juliet just for a moment.] Chemistry though, goes way beyond a special sexual connection. When two people "connect" in all areas; sexually, minds, personalities and their hearts all connect forming the greatest companionship. In general, it is what the goal of dating is all about.

Chemistry is something very powerful. It is what draws us to one person, even if we hardly know them. But there is actual scientific research that shows just how we may be attracted to one particular person, but not another. Why we feel some people are more attractive than others and how our minds actually play more of a role than our hearts do when it comes to love. What it all boils down to is biochemistry.

Neuroscientists, Ingrid Olson and Christy Marshuetz, devised a sneaky experiment to answer the question, "How long does it take to decide if a person is hot?"

They exposed men and women to a series of per-rated faces, some knockouts and others of average appearance, then asked them to rate the appearances of all the faces they saw. The twist was that the faces flickered on the screen for only thirteen milliseconds- (a flash so fast you'd swear that you did not see anything at all!) Without knowing why they gave good looking faces significantly higher scores, the implication here is that beauty is perceived subconsciously. They didn't have time to meditate on anyone's "hotness," therefore, judging attractiveness seems to happen just as automatically as judging age and expression.

When you see an attractive face, rewards centers of your brain known as the nucleus encumbers and orbitofrontal cortex are stimulated as well as the amygdala, which captures expression. We also have a specialized cortical network knows as the fuisform facial area, which in an instant, may process a person's entire face. It takes coordination between these areas of the brain, including the temporal and occipital lobes of the right hemisphere, to form a complete impression of a person's appearance. [Source: Jena Pincott]

So, if you think about it- Hollywood isn't choosing who is "hot," our brains are choosing them for us. Each one of us has the capacity to think alike and also think differently.

Peer pressure in society makes us all believe that someone could be "hot" when in reality we may not really find that particular person is as attractive as Hollywood thinks.

But what I find even more interesting than talking about "chemistry," is the fact that the more wiggle in a woman's walk, the tinier your waist is in proportion to your hips, which is a telltale sign of youth and fertility. The way you move is called sexual appeal. A woman's waist-to-hip ratio is one of the MOST important cues in sexual attraction. The smaller your waist is in proportion to your hips, the curvier you appear. There's evidence that men prefer women with a low WHR (waist hip measurement) because curves mean smarter kids.

Note to all you ladies who look to be a size 0 – The more curves you have the smarter kids you will birth. So, maybe, just maybe that diet you want to try so you are like all the photo-shopped models you see on Instagram, isn't what you should be striving for.

And just as I conclude this book, a recent Pew Research study found that more people believe online dating has had a negative impact on dating and relationships than a positive one, and that people still think relationships that start in person are more likely to succeed than those that start online.

Roughly seven-in-ten online daters believe it is very common for those who use these platforms to lie to try to appear more desirable. And by a wide margin, Americans who have used a dating site or app in the past year say the experience left them feeling more frustrated (45%) than hopeful (28%).

A clear majority of online daters (71%) say it is very common for people on these platforms to lie about themselves to appear more desirable, while another 25% think it is somewhat common. Only 3% of online daters think this is not a common occurrence on dating platforms.

Smaller, but still substantial shares, of online daters believe people setting up fake accounts in order to scam others (50%) or people receiving sexually explicit messages or images they did not ask for (48%) are very common on dating sites and apps. By contrast, online daters are less likely to think harassment or bullying, and privacy violations, such as data breaches or identify theft, are very common occurrences on these platforms.

You cannot filter your way into a perfect relationship. That takes real effort. And, perhaps most of all, we now are realizing that being obsessed with looking for "hot singles" is not the best approach online or even offline for that matter.

Most dating apps force users to make decisions based on nothing more than a headshot. While that may work for those who are on the app for a hook-up, it does not work for long-term relationships.

Let me also add that us girls do not friend-zone you guys because you are "nice." We friend-zone you simply because we are not attracted to you nor have common interests therefore we don't want to date you. It has nothing to do with y ou being nice. Trust me, we want to me with nice guys. All the guys online are harping that we don't want a nice guy. They are fooling themselves!

If you want to really be in a serious relationship, then the bottom line is this: you need to stop this nonsense in thinking that dating apps are going to be the place where you are going to meet him/her.

Stop forcing relationships to happen.
Stop trying so hard.

Go out into the world and pay attention to what is happening around you. There are people out there wanting to meet someone like you. Be patient. Relationships are not a destination, there are a journey and know this:

At some point in life, someone will love you more than what you've expected. Be patient and learn to wait, because sometimes, a patient person receives the best love story.

BONUS COVERAGE:

It maybe news to some, but Athletes, Social Media, and Dating Apps don't really mix.

Athletes show me time and time again, that they really don't "get" the power of social media and what it truly is good for. They either tweet the stupidest of things like;

rap lyrics, content that is created for their brand that really has no purpose, telling everyone they have "moved on" from a situation when in fact they haven't, responding to the press in a tweet that makes no sense, social issues, RTing crap, or my favorite, other celebrities and athletes.

These athletes don't release the power of the platform. They all "claim" that they have a platform, but they misuse it every single time.

Social media is possibly one of the most powerful tools of the 21st century. Social media provides an avenue for athletes to not only engage with fans, but also influence them with the right content that helps fans make a decision. It's also a great way to highlight inspirational stories and get people pumped up! Too bad they don't know this and they listen to their agents, PR folks and other people in their camps on what to post and those people are not educated on this topic at all!

They miss the boat on what exactly social media can do for them besides gaining sponsorships with corporations. First and foremost it is called "Social Media" not Anti-social media. Most professional athletes fail to connect with actual people and just respond to other celebrities and athletes. They could in turn learn a lot from just connecting online with fans that support them! Just a little response like, "Thank you for your support- it means a lot..." and then add a teams hashtag would make that connection to the fan base even stronger.

The next reason to use social media as an athlete would be to inspire or motivate others. There is the 80/20 rule that most don't follow and that is 80% of your content should be motivating, inspiring, fun, educating and engaging and 20% sell. This goes for EVERY business using social media, not just athletes. Most athletes miss the opportunity to use social media to tell their own story- where they grew up, how they got to where they are, etc. **On social media an athlete can tell a real-life story with ups and downs, comebacks, setbacks, tests and triumphs.**

It's not all glamorous.

Here's what I rarely see athletes do: They don't **Show themselves in action both on and off the field of play**: While it's important to show how they compete, they decide to post pictures of waiting at airports, training in the gym, getting on a bus, etc. They don't **let Their personality shine**: Many athletes are so scared of social media controversy that they edit their accounts down to the point that they feel inauthentic; fake people, not keeping it real. **Remember, personality can't be photo-shopped.**

The most popular social media accounts feel authentic. There's no robot posting for them, hence why I can't stand it when athletes and celebrities let their PR department, who knows squat about social media, post for them. They don't hire the correct people to bring out the realness of the person, so it feels as if a robot is If else you may lose your followers in translation. And then here's a fact about athletes and men in general.

Men love to post about "their" woman because they are proud of who they're with- it's an ego thing. Men also want other men to know – "She's mine, so back off," and keep the other guys in place.

Then there are athletes, who don't want other women to know that they are exclusive, so they don't post simply because they don't want to leave a trail that they are dating someone to make it easier to hook up with other females. And the MAIN excuse you will hear from these guys is, "I want to keep my life private," or, "It's no one's business who I am with and what I am doing."

Then there are athletes today who are VERY good having their cake and eating it too. (a cliche but true in this case) Have you heard the term "stashing"? It's when your partner hides you from their virtual world by avoiding all interactions between you on social media.

Here's what it looks like:

They upload pics of the meal you shared, but don't tag you and only write generic descriptions like: "delicious food!"

They post a pic of your favorite band's concert, but your name is nowhere to be seen in the description.

You find an awesome meme about their favorite film and tag them, but they never answer.

He likes his friends' pics but doesn't react to yours.

You choose a pic of the two of you as your profile pic and tag them; they never approve the tag.

They post comments on other people's posts, but never on yours.

They don't see your Instagram stories (although they appear in most of them).

They -occasionally- like pics of you, but only where you appear with other people.

They "forget" to post the pic where the two of you appear together.

At first glance, it may seem irrelevant, or maybe you think that there is no reason to be alarmed, since what you live in real life with that person is more valuable. However, it does matter, and it is painful.

If your partner isn't even going to respect you on a PUBLIC platform, what is he going to do in private?

When athletes seek attention on social media, they are basically proving that for them, image and external validation take precedence over authenticity, substance, maturity, and connection. And what is life without any of those?

It's a red flag when they are consistently looking for attention *outside* of a relationship on Instagram, Tinder, and other social apps. And trust me, MANY professional athletes are out there hooking up with girls that either have slid into their Dms or they have found on dating apps. Moreover, it is concerning because most of these guys have either a girlfriend, wife, or a child with a woman who they are "supposedly" connected to but on social media there is no trace of this relationship at all.

When someone asks if you're seeing anyone, no one expects you to whip out a flash drive with a PowerPoint presentation of "The Entire History of Me & My One True

Love." But acting as if you are single when you're not is sketchy as hell.

Another red flag that I see a lot is the fact that it gets weird when you start untagging yourself from photos and status updates your partner posts.

Like everything else in a relationship, communication is important here — if you don't like *any* photos of you to appear on social media, just tell your partner. If you don't, it just looks like you're trying to bury evidence that you're together.

Also note, If you are NOT a couple, you then, therefore do NOT take a couple's picture together with other couples. (Like Sam Darnold did a few months ago)

Sometimes an athlete blends in with the other folk on dating apps, and well, sometimes they don't.

Former Toronto Raptors guard Greivis Vasquez, (He is now a basketball coach, since he can't play after he had surgery on his right ankle.) was hoping that he could just blend in with the millions of others on Tinder without actually getting recognized.

That wasn't the case, though, as Vasquez was spotted on the app, prior to a game in Philadelphia, no doubt looking for a little love on the road.

And there are MANY MANY other athletes that use Tinder for just that: Nooky on the road. I will go into depth about the New York Jets player, other NFL players, NBA players and even NHL players who are on Tinder.

I will tell you the dating apps where all the athletes are; and there are some new ones that were created just for them, as we see a rise in dating apps that are centered around certain professions and hobbies.

I will discuss the controversy surrounding the ability to see a person's criminal record while swiping on potential love interests now on Tinder. And... I will talk about the app Raya; where Matthew Perry and Ben Affleck were found out to be using to message young women.

I will also reveal the best spy apps -if your heart is into this. One of them allows you to spy on folks IG messages. Now, that can be dangerous. But it also can be eye opening to know that there are folks out there that do this stuff and to be smarter when it comes to using this technology. I also will tell you HOW you can FIND EVERY single ATHLETE using Tinder!! There is a formula for it!

Where will I reveal all this information?

In the bonus section in the second dating journal that will be released in a few weeks. I also will have some personal stuff – but in the meantime, here are some helpful social media tips that you use immediately.

If you would be embarrassed to share something with your grandma, you probably shouldn't post it. There is also this rule that if you have a social media account, there is truly no point to keeping it private. I get the fact that you don't want strangers just commenting left and right, but the point of posting "secretive" stuff... I never and still don't get why you would do that. Keep in mind the photos that you thought could only be seen for a few seconds can be photographed or turned into a screenshot and come back to haunt you weeks later.

Social media is a living resume that showcases your character. The things that make you authentically YOU. And at the same time, social media can be used against you as I just mentioned above.

Posting criminal activities or conspiring with other social media members to riot, protest or loot can also be used as evidence against you.

If you intend to show people that you are rude, it shows it. If you intend to show people that you are nasty, it shows it. If you intend to show people that you are a complete asshole, it show it too.

The internet leaves a trail everywhere for everyone. The trouble with the internet is that you're never *entirely* sure of who you're speaking with online. Anyone who's seen *Catfish* - already knows this. So, for that reason, think twice about engaging in direct/ private conversations online, *especially* if the other party starts asking for private details.

Unless you know for a fact who you are speaking to, never give out your email, phone number, address, credit card or banking information in DMS- ever!

Finally, if you want to follow me on social media, reach out to me for advice or tips you can find me here:

Instagram: @sassygirlpr7

Twitter: SweetStephanie7

Pinterest: SassyProductions7

Facebook: Sassy Style Brand (StephanieDolce)

My personal Facebook to follow:
https://www.facebook.com/stephanie.dolce.98 (This is where I do my radio show "The Sassy Show" LIVE each week. (usually on Thursdays 3pm EST)

More to come.